TO GROW YOUR SMALL BUSINESS

ROD SLOANE WITHDRAWN

121 Marketing Ideas to Grow Your Small Business
© 2007 by **Roderick Sloane**

Cover Design: **Jaquetta Trueman**, www.wakethetiger.com
Book Design & Typesetting: **Jaquetta Trueman**

Text set in Abadi Light 11 on 15pt

First published in 2007 by **Ecademy Press**
6 Woodland Rise, Penryn, Cornwall, UK. TR10 8QD
Info@ecademy-press.com. www.ecademy-press.com

Printed and bound by **Lightning Source**
in the UK and USA

*Printed on acid-free paper from managed forests. This book is
printed on demand, so no copies will be remaindered or pulped.*

ISBN 1-905823-12-6
    978-1-905823-12-3

Other Publications by Rod Sloane

The Special Report Collection:

How to Attract Profitable New Clients

Advanced Referral Strategies for Law Firms CD

How to Attract Profitable New Clients to your Law Firm's Web Site CD

Attracting Profitable New Clients Live!' 6-CD Album

Acknowledgments

Thanks to all those that have influenced me, these include:

My parents, brothers & sister, the staff at Blackpool Grammar School, all the people I have met at BNI, ToastMasters, NSA, and PSA.

Special thanks go to my wife Mary and daughter Kerry.

This book is dedicated to the memory of my father,
P.J Sloane

Contents

About the author

Rod Sloane

Rod is a marketing coach, seminar leader, author and professional speaker. His company (www.RodSloane. co.uk) helps small business owners to overcome their discomfort with marketing and take their business to the next level. He believes in "no bull, no nonsense marketing that simply works".

After graduating with an Economics Degree from the University of Portsmouth, he spent 15 years working in corporate sales and marketing with IBM, BAT and Computer Associates. He has spent the last ten years in business development with professional services firms.

Born and schooled in Blackpool, Lancashire, he now lives with his wife and daughter in Ealing, West London.

Marketing is a system, not an event.

John Jantsch – Author of Duct Tape Marketing – The World's Most Practical Small Business Marketing Guide

Small business marketers love the chase. Love the new-fangled way to make the phone ring. They love to think of a marketing promotion as a single event. It's precisely this view of marketing that holds most small businesses back. They fall prey to the "marketing idea of the week" and never fully explore what it takes to create and build a completely functioning, consistently performing, marketing system.

It's funny how many small business owners can think of things such as finance and operations as a system but, when it comes to marketing, all bets are off. Marketing is a system. Marketing is one of the most important systems. This book will get you started with a new way to think about marketing your business.

Effective marketing is little more than creating and operating an effective marketing system. Now, when I use the word system I mean several things.

1) The system is documented – You can't have a system or a step in a system unless you write it down.
2) The system is built on sound marketing principles and
3) You constantly measure, innovate, and refine the system.

This little book is a collection of solid strategies and tactics. My advice to you dear reader is that you pick out a number of the tips in this book and string together your very own marketing system. Stick with it, do something every day, week and month and eventually you find that you've build a high-powered marketing machine.

Okay ... now the last bit of advice.

Every system needs a champion. Either find someone in your organisation who does little else but operate the system or hire a marketing professional and charge them with helping you develop, implement and run the system.

Properly fed and maintained, this little marketing system can become the engine that drives your firm's climb to the top.

Introduction

If you really mean business, well then, this is one book you need to take seriously. And that means it's time to sit up and take notice very, very keenly – because this is the kind of book that could be a Bible to someone like you, if you are interested in expanding your business.

In other words, this is no time for lounging around and taking it easy if you are serious about learning the tricks of the trade. So get ready to mark off the points that interest you so that you can find them easily should you need to refer to them again.

Treat this book as a personal handbook and jot down anything that comes to mind. You can write in the margins, underscore wherever you want and do just about anything else, because this book is yours to treat as you like. And that also means that you should not consider lending it to anyone, even if you think they would find it useful.

In fact, should you come across anyone who would be interested in reading the book, do get them another copy or encourage them to get one themselves because by the time you are through with yours, it will be of little use to anyone else. Apart from anything else, your jottings etc. will have given it a unique character of its own, along with your personal touch.

And then again, don't forget that your friend, acquaintance or colleague who may have expressed interest in the book may not want to read it for the same reasons that you do. They may have a completely different outlook – all the more reason for getting their own copies.

This is one book you are unlikely to put down until you have read it through. So go right ahead and find out everything you need to know about expanding your own small business. Find out how to get started, the diverse issues involved, the pitfalls to avoid etc. so that by the time you get going, you will be confident that you have all the know-how you need to make your enterprise a total success. Good luck and happy reading!!

1. Be Sure That You Excel in Your Field

This is probably the first prerequisite to taking up any kind of enterprise, offering a service, promoting a product or setting up a business of your own. After all, you can never forget that whatever it is you are attempting to do, there are so many others who are in the same boat. The result is competition – competition that is getting more and more cut-throat by the day as more and more products, services and technologies are launched in the never-ending quest for excellence.

Just think – let's say you are really committed to bringing out a product that is the ultimate in that particular field. If this is the same train of thought of even a few others in the same field, it's really going to be uphill work to prove that you are the best when there are so many people doing the same thing.

In this sea of ever increasing competition that has engulfed practically every product and service in existence, with new ones constantly emerging, you will need to be really good at whatever you do. Only then will you be able to make your mark and be remembered. Only then will yours be the name that will come to mind when that particular product or service is in demand.

2. Formulate a Marketing Strategy

Devising a marketing strategy is vital to the success of your small business. However, that does not mean that such a plan should be long and convoluted. The simplest plans are the most effective and you would do well to formulate one of your own. And remember to keep it short and concise.

The highlight of your plan should be the objectives that you hope to achieve within six months. You could follow that up with a more detailed breakdown of how you propose to accomplish these objectives.

It would probably help to divide your time frame into segments of 30 days each. Make sure your plan is visible so that it serves as a constant reminder to you of the targets you have set yourself. Make out one such plan for your department and make sure there's a copy available for everyone who draws a salary.

The effectiveness of your strategy will be largely responsible for determining the success of your business. Plan well and you will be able to reap the benefits. When plans go wrong, chaos is often the result. With a little care, you can avoid such calamities and sail through smoothly. And remember, as the saying goes, the proof of the pudding is in the eating!

3. State your business clearly

The way you present yourself is vital to your image and to your eventual success in your chosen field. Therefore it would be a good idea to consider which would be the most effective way to introduce yourself and your business. The idea naturally would be to make a lasting impression on the listener.

If you choose to introduce yourself by way of the service you offer, well so do thousands of others. It does not make you come across as being in any way distinctive.

Often the best way to do this is to go by the results you have achieved with your clients. And the best way you can achieve that is to ask yourself what your clients are looking for. In short, you need to find out what your clients need from you. They will either be looking to maximise their returns or to cut their losses.

And then again, do remember to keep your manner and your replies to enquiries as conversational as possible. Offer the kind of replies that people will feel free to repeat if they need to. Such replies will have a power of their own.

When you are able to give a direct response to queries about the nature of your work, you are more likely to draw the kind of clients you want. With this kind of approach, you will also be in a better position to come to a better understanding with new clients.

4. Brush up your marketing know-how

If you are going to be setting up a business, you need to be absolutely sure that you have your facts right. And that's not all. You need to be aware of all the intricacies involved – and have the necessary knowledge at your fingertips, because you never know what you might be up against.

So the best thing you can do is to read up as much as you can on the subject. Acquaint yourself as thoroughly as possible with relevant issues, and do take into account the opinions and experiences of experts in the field.

As mentioned in the foreword of this book, apart from reading it, treat the book as a kind of workbook – your very own, in which you can feel free to write, jot points, make notes, underscore etc. Highlight the sections that interest you in particular.

As for the kind of books you should buy, you would do well to review your situation after you have been through this book. Look at the kind of knowledge you have gained from it and its relevance to your intention of expanding your business.

You can then take the opinions of friends, colleagues and booksellers as to the direction you should take in terms of reference material. When you have found the kind of book you are looking for, treasure it, read it thoroughly and derive as much from it as you can. Once you are through, for good measure, read it again.

Your second reading will make all the difference, as all the matters you have imbibed will fall into place.

5. Engage a consultant

When you are starting out on a new venture, what could be more reassuring than the availability of advice from an experienced person – someone who can offer guidance on how you should proceed with your venture, what to expect and look out for, possible difficulties etc. and how to get around them.

Occasionally, a consultant may turn up an excellent idea, which could leave you wondering why you never thought of it yourself. The fact is that you are too closely involved in the process of setting up your enterprise. Sometimes, this kind of situation can prevent you from seeing what is staring you in the face. That is where your consultant comes in.

Your consultant can also prove how valuable he is to you by asking you the right questions – questions that will initiate a thought process for you. That can make all the difference to the decisions you take and the course you take in the way forward.

Ideally, the kind of person you should look out for should be an individual who is a good listener, is capable of asking thought-provoking questions and thinking through various options to assist you to arrive at the best possible decision pertaining to your situation.

You may wonder how to go about finding such a person. Well, you could take the easy way out and simply check out the prospects with a colleague or acquaintance that has turned up ideas that appealed to you.

6. Do not depend on your Marketing Division

When you are in need of ideas to promote your business, do remember that the primary responsibility for the success or failure of your project lies with you. Marketing may achieve a great deal to promote your enterprise, but it's the decisions that you take that will impact the outcome.

It's the way you project yourself and your business that will ultimately produce results. Marketing and business development personnel merely assist you in doing what you must do for yourself. They are waiting in the wings, so to speak. It's you who will really have to go out there and make an impact to draw attention and attract clients to your business.

Of course, this does not mean that they do not have a significant role to play. After all, marketing people are expected to provide a structure that will give you direction. They are in a position to give you valuable suggestions and guidance on critical issues, all of which is invaluable in terms of assistance.

But despite everything, the major decisions that will have a bearing on your ability to attract clients will have to be taken by you and you alone. It's a major responsibility; you should be certain that you are ready to shoulder it.

7. Attract your clients with informative reports

Just think about this – you are looking to attract clients to your new small business. You'd better be sure that what you have to offer them is attractive enough to arouse their interest. One of the ways in which you can accomplish this is by writing reports on pertinent issues with a view to educating your reader.

Such articles targeting people who are trying to set up new business ventures are sure to attract interest. This kind of interest will ultimately be focussed on you and your business aspirations.

Capture the interest of would be clients by addressing issues that you know would be vital to them. Much of this will depend on the kind of business that you are looking to set up. For example, if you are concerned with interior decoration, any articles you write on the subject are sure to draw the attention of like-minded people. These people may well turn out to become your future clients.

Select your subjects carefully and make your articles concise and focussed. Be practical and stick to the point, dealing specifically with the subject you are trying to discuss. Take tips on format from the kind of leaflets that are available in supermarkets, and you should be on the right track.

8. Promote your reports

Once you have brought out a special report of your own, you need to think about how you are going to market it. For starters, to attract interest, you need to have a catchy title. Your choice of title will naturally depend on what would appeal to your clients.

Although special reports of this kind are more often called White Papers, you may decide to stick with the term Special Report, depending on how it suits your particular purpose. A Special Report is typically a concise document of not more than 20 pages, written for the purpose of solving problems that people in your chosen field and situation may come up against.

So if you write up a good report you could well turn up a winner. Offer solutions to problems and clients will come flocking to you! And that naturally, is what you want.

You may choose to give away your Special Report. Alternatively, you could also use it as a kind of bait to draw the attention of prospective clients to your online newsletter. And then again, you can even market your report by posting it on your website.

Once you have done that, it would help to provide hyperlinks to your website in your Special Report. While you may find that many people will be satisfied to read your reports online, there may be others who would like to take a look at the hard copy. So do be sure that you carry some of these around with you when you are out meeting people and trying to establish contacts.

9. Create a website of your own

In these modern times, this is one step you should know would be to your advantage, no matter what your business is concerned with. This is the most efficient way to get your message across and have prospective clients get back to you with queries, problems, suggestions etc.

You may still argue that a website is not really necessary, particularly if you have succeeded in spreading the word without one. But make no mistake; you need that website if you really want to be an effective operator. Suppose you have managed to communicate everything you wanted to by word of mouth, through personal meetings etc. You may not think so, but you will still need to use a website. Apart from communicating efficiently with your prospective clients, your website will also be instrumental in projecting your image as a professional operator.

New clients may want to find out more about you once they have come across some information about you or the services you offer. It would never do for you to be unavailable online, would it?

Your website would also be a useful medium for communicating all the information that would otherwise have gone into printed brochures – far more economical and convenient than sending out printed matter to a large number of people.

Also, your information would be available online for anyone who chose to view it. In other words, you can reach any number of people and have them get back to you in no time at all – at a fraction of the cost that printed communication would entail.

You could also make alterations more easily on your website. And don't forget that a website gives you the opportunity to present your matter in creative ways that will be more interesting to prospective clients. For example, you could put in audio features, to give clients the feeling that they are dealing with active communication. It could make a world of difference to their response.

10. Using a website to manage your business

Managing your business through the use of a website can be very rewarding in opening up a number of possibilities for you. For one thing, it is flexible and you can market just about anything through your website, regardless of what the product or service is.

For instance, you may need to send out different kinds of mailings at different frequencies to customers of different categories. You can do so with comparative ease through your website. You can generate a significant amount of revenue by marketing your products online.

Websites offer an opportunity to identify prospective clients and target them. Once you have identified them, you can concentrate on sending them the bulk of your communication since you regard them as your most valued clients. Communication with them will then take precedence over others.

Mix and Match

You can even use a combination of marketing through your database and telemarketing. In fact, you could go still further by using email and the Web to get your message across.

However, if you do decide to proceed in this way, do remember that you will have to take into account any legal restrictions that may apply with regard to unsolicited mail, etc. You could land yourself in trouble if you are not careful.

11. Bring out a newsletter

In seeking to expand your small business, you may find that publishing a newsletter can have far reaching results. Newsletters make a handy tool because people are generally receptive to them and look to them for new ideas. Newsletters can be informative, apart from being instrumental in building customer loyalty.

Once you have a client following, you cannot assume that you can always depend on their patronage just because they opted for your products once before. You can use a newsletter to keep your clients informed of product developments, special offers, other news etc. It's pretty likely that as long as they keep hearing from you, you will keep hearing from them.

You can use your newsletter to turn your clients into vehicles of publicity. In other words, when you have clients who favour your products, you can capitalise on their loyalty by getting them to spread the word about your product or service. These are people who will stand by you and encourage everyone they know to do the same!

You can also use newsletters to popularise the versatility of your products by highlighting how you can get the best out of them or how other customers have found additional uses for them. A newsletter is a great way to publicise the performance of successful products to prospective clients.

12. Improve your selling skills

Do remember that the more successful you are at selling your products, the more you will directly benefit your business. It is therefore definitely worth taking the trouble to investigate how you can maximise your sales.

This is one of the most critical decisions you will have to make and the results will be directly reflected in the performance of your business. You can choose to sell by using a blend of different sales models.

This means that you can engage a large company to sell your products. Alternatively, you can hire independent sales people, manufacturers' representatives or telemarketing personnel.

Using the sales resources of another company can work well, particularly if you are the owner of a small product based enterprise. If you can get a distributor with an independent sales force, you will be able to promote your product effectively. You could also use manufacturers' representatives, but you would have to work hard to convince them about the selling potential of your products.

If you were to hire sales people from outside, you would have to keep a close watch on them. It's usually simpler to hire effective telemarketing personnel who are able to present well. Your first priority should be to concentrate on the customer and his needs.

While you may be very keen to show off your products and describe them at length to the customer, you will have to stop yourself short and remember that the customer's needs at that particular time must come first.

13. Making presentations

When you are making a presentation with the idea of expanding your small business, it's important to remember that appearances count —and that begins with the way you present yourself. There are many different kinds of presentations, such as first encounters, sales presentations, interviews and briefings, to name a few. The one you choose will depend largely on the kind of audience you are facing. So also will the way you present.

You can take any of a number of approaches in interacting with your audience. The most effective of these is to come straight to the point and say what you have to say. Be sure to capture the attention of your audience, so that you can build a rapport quickly.

And how would you do that? Well, it has everything to do with what you are trying to tell your audience and how you go about it. Once you get into the spirit of things, humour, intonation, gestures etc, will do a great deal to contribute to the nature of your presentation. Of course, you must take into account that the way you will come across to a room full of people will be quite different to the way you will come across to a smaller group.

14. Speaking skills

Speaking to an audience is an excellent opportunity for you to make direct contact with the people you are trying to reach. It's also an opportunity to make the best possible impression in person. So make the most of it and play your cards right. While it takes time for any kind of relationship to develop, you can also build a relationship with an audience, even one comprised of strangers, in the space of half an hour or so.

This is where emotional intelligence comes in – the capacity to see things from the other person's point of view. If you can do that, you will probably be able to gauge their behaviour and foresee the kind of reactions they may have. The audience you are facing will naturally be interested in the element of 'What's In It for me' or WIIFM, as it is commonly known.

Empathy and intuition play a major part here. Understanding where they are coming from and being able to relate to them accordingly will have a great deal to do with the way you deliver your talk – and the impact you make. People with highly developed skills of this kind are likely to achieve greater success.

15. Advertising in the right places

Advertising has everything to do with publicising your expanding business. The way you advertise your products can make all the difference to the response you get from your clients. This will also be a reflection of how the product or products will be received in the wider market.

To advertise effectively, you need to target the publications you know your clients will be interested in. You could also use radio or television advertising. The best way to obtain publicity for your product is to position it in a way that makes it attractive and unique compared to the products being offered by your competitors.

You will do well to remember that you need to review your expenditure on media costs. If you are considering print advertising, you should know that advertisement rates for print media are fixed. This is because print media enjoys the flexibility of being able to turn out copies of the publication depending on demand.

You can make use of promotional offers, which are very effective in drawing the attention of clients to your business. You have seen them in action often enough; isn't it time to get them to work for you? It's certainly worth thinking about.

16. Stay abreast of technology

In these modern times, the success of your expanding business will depend largely on how conversant you are with technological advances in communication. Word can get around really fast these days if you can get comfortable with the latest technologies.

Make it a point to learn how to market and operate your business on the web. Get accustomed to the terminology and learn everything you can about e-commerce and advertising your products online.

Study the implications of e-commerce for your expanding business. You can really benefit from the facilities offered by the Internet and digital technology, particularly if you are looking to economise. Service providers and vendors are constantly trying to promote low cost services.

Applications are the order of the day in this digital age and you will have to get comfortable with acronyms such as "wysiwyg" or 'what you see is what you get' – a style that will give you the freedom to create the kind of website you want, depending on how you plan to project your business.

Application service providers have also become popular and you can use them to advantage to acquire applications off the shelf that you feel would be useful in running your business.

17. Install a suggestion box for employees

This is one idea you really must make use of because you must remember that it is your employees that make your business what it is. It's therefore really important that you get feedback from them about issues concerning them.

As an employer, it is vital that you maintain an interest in the welfare of your employees. You can empty the suggestion box from time to time and have an open discussion with your staff. You may even find that they will give you some good ideas that you would like to implement.

A suggestion box will also make you aware of any problems they may be facing. You can then give some thought to ways and means around those problems. Above all, a suggestion box will give your staff the message that you are interested in them as people and not just as workers who get the job done.

Encouraging them to put their suggestions in the box will tell them, as nothing else can, that they count, and that you are interested in what they have to say. A good interaction between you and your employees will pay off in the long run, fostering employee loyalty and strengthening the foundation of your business.

18. Accumulate email addresses

This again is just another way of keeping up with the times. You may be really busy in the course of expanding your business. You may be meeting any number of people each day in various places that you are required to visit. Some you may have a reason to remember, others you may not.

Taking the step of keeping email addresses is a wise move because you never know when you may need to contact someone again. It is much simpler to store email addresses on your computer than to keep track of mailing addresses, although you may need those from time to time as well.

Email messages offer a quick and simple way to communicate with people regardless of where they are. This of course is not the case with mailing addresses, apart from the fact that sending mail by post takes time. So wherever you go, do make sure that you keep collecting email addresses from your contacts.

Asking for email addresses will also automatically send the message that you are both up to date and comfortable with modern methods of communication. This will also reflect on the efficiency of your business. You can store everything on a laptop and carry it with you wherever you go.

19. Put yourself in your client's shoes

To really understand what a client expects from your business, try putting yourself in his place. Consider that you are an individual looking at your business from the outside and try to see it with a fresh perspective. Picture yourself as a client and consider what you would be seeking from a business of this kind.

This could start a thought process that may turn up surprising results, shedding light on aspects of your business that perhaps had not occurred to you before. Thinking about your business from the client's point of view can only be a positive experience, even if it makes you aware of certain negatives.

So do put yourself through this exercise from time to time. It is possible to get so caught up in running a business that you may not see a flaw that is staring you in the face. It's a good way to take care of both sides of the matter.

20. Humility pays

No matter how successful you have been in expanding your business, remember that there is always room for improvement. Your business is made up of so many facets that it is unlikely that you will have thought of everything at any given time.

What's more, you may even find that ideas for improvement can come from unexpected quarters. Regardless of how well you may have thought things through, it's always wise to be open to the possibility that something could have been done better. More important, be humble enough to recognise that changes are required and should be carried through if they are important enough to the performance of your business.

The changes could extend from alterations in your style of functioning to changes in attitude, changes in policy matters to just about anything else. Remember that nobody's perfect and you are no exception. The sooner you recognise that, the more receptive you will be to the need for change as and when it does arise.

Being seen as receptive to change also sends a message to your colleagues and employees that you are flexible. This is far better than clamming up, and giving the impression of being rigid in your outlook. This kind of flexibility can only be an asset, both for your business and in your personal interactions.

21. Sending thank you cards

Sending thank you cards to colleagues, associates and employees speaks volumes for the kind of person you are. Apart from anything else, it projects appreciation as well as humility and gives you one more reason to interact pleasantly with the person or organisation concerned. All of which does plenty to keep relations cordial.

You can have your thank you cards personalised with name of your company and a message printed inside the card. The flap of the envelope could carry your return address as well as your company logo. Such cards could be sent to clients whose custom you value. You could also send thank you cards in appreciation of good work.

Thank you cards tell people that you do not take them or the things they do for granted. This will ultimately project a favourable image of your business. Taking a little trouble over such things can go a long way to building loyalty in corporate relationships.

And ultimately, you could even send thank you cards to your own employees in appreciation of their good work, as and when the occasion arises. This will remind them that they are important to you. It will also be clear to them that you value their contribution to your business.

22. Use the Yellow Pages

You can advertise effectively in the Yellow Pages if you want to spread the word about your expanding business. However, it would be wise to remember that competition will be very stiff among the different contenders in a particular field.

You could say the Yellow Pages are the ultimate in advertising through print media. Here you will find a comprehensive listing of companies concerned with just about any product or service.

Yellow Pages advertising differ from other varieties of print advertising in that it is sold annually. You can get a basic one line listing with your commercial telephone service. You can then make changes depending on how you want the advertisement to appear. This would include the size of the advertisement, your choice of type, addition of colour, emphasis etc.

The cost would naturally depend on the kind of advertisement or listing you opt for – for example, listing in a small town would be relatively inexpensive when compared with listing in a metropolitan area.

Even if you do decide to advertise through the Yellow Pages, you can back up the advertisement with other kinds of publicity. Remember that it's important for clients to recognise and remember your name. That by itself could make a world of difference to your commercial standing, and of course, to your competitive edge.

23. Ask for feedback from your existing clients

The volume of your existing clientele is evidence enough of the level of efficiency of your small business. Even so, you could get a better idea of how clients view your business if you asked them for feedback on your performance.

From such information you would be getting opinions directly from your clients, which you must treat as extremely valuable. It's an indication of how your business is actually viewed by the people or organisations you serve.

You may find that all the news you get through this kind of feedback is not always what you want to hear. For example, it may come to light that one aspect or another of your performance may not always have satisfied clients. However, in such a situation, you should consider even such 'negative' revelations as valuable.

You may ask 'Why?' The answer is because you are getting an opportunity to identify deficiencies in your performance, which you can then rectify. The end result of this is that you will be able to deliver better value to your clients.

In the same way, positive feedback from your clients will serve to enhance your own confidence in those areas. After all, you have got your news straight from the horse's mouth!!

24. Ask for feedback from former clients

You will no doubt be faced with the situation of having had clients who have left you and moved on. It would be well worth the trouble to find out what it was that caused them to make the change.

Again, you have to accept that you may not always like what you find out. But then, facts are facts and you have to face them. So you may as well take the plunge! And don't assume that this is necessarily going to be a negative or demoralising experience.

You may find out plenty from your former clients that will work to your advantage. What they have to tell you could well open your eyes to aspects of your business or performance that can be improved.

There may be a number of factors that you have, for some reason, failed to take into account. Your former clients, in moving on, may have found something in the new services they opted for that was missing in yours.

Look at the bright side, learn from your mistakes and capitalise on the experience of your competitors in the market. All is not lost just because your services were found wanting in certain areas. Far from it! In fact, you could say you are on the threshold of a whole new experience.

25. Make business cards available to all your staff

Your business card is a statement in itself – a statement of what you do and how well you do it. The people on your staff are very much a part of your business and you want them to know that their contribution is important.

So do make sure that you let them know how much they matter to you. One of the ways in which you can do this is to make sure that they all carry business cards.

When you do that, you are letting them know that you value them. As they go about their business, in contact with various people, those people will also get the message about the regard you have for your staff. This again will speak volumes about your organisation – and ultimately about you.

When all your staff members are equipped with business cards, your clients or prospective clients will know that they can approach anyone in your organisation with their queries and get reliable responses.

Making sure your staff carry business cards will also tell the people they interact with that your organisation is one in which everybody has a significant role to play – a role that you have taken the trouble to acknowledge.

26. Stay in touch with your clients

As the owner of a small but expanding business, your clients are vitally important to you. You could say this is true of all clients because, to a large extent, clients make a business what it is. But it is even more important from the point of view of an expanding business.

Since this is so, you should take care to give your clients the attention they deserve. You can do this by keeping in regular touch with them, say once a week. It helps to maintain good relations with them.

Remember that your clients could also spread the word about your expanding business. If they have been happy with the service they have received from you, you will probably find that they will recommend your services to friends, relatives and acquaintances. All of which will be free publicity for you, with plenty of goodwill thrown in.

The more attention you give your clients, the more likely they are to stay on with you. Since they are also people on the move, you will also get titbits of news about developments in the market – news that may be pretty handy if you are looking to make improvements to your business.

27. Think success

Doing well begins with thinking positively. If you have a positive outlook, you are much more likely to make a success of your business, whatever your field may be.

While it may not always come naturally to see yourself as successful, the more you try to train yourself to think that way, the more likely you are to make it a reality.

Feeling that you can succeed is naturally a good, positive feeling. Just try to visualise how you would feel if you were to see yourself in a negative light. Now that is hardly the way you can expect to feel good about yourself or anything you are planning to do.

So the more you can get yourself to think positively, the better you will feel about the projects you undertake. And when you are trying to expand your business, that positive feeling is something you cannot do without.

In fact, as far as your business is concerned, nothing could be more important to your survival than this positive feeling. If you make up your mind that you are going to succeed, in all probability you will make every effort to see that you do. Sink into the depths of despair and you can hardly expect to get very far. So it's up to you to take the right approach.

28. Advertise through search engines

Search engines can be powerful tools through which you can publicise your expanding business. This kind of advertising sometimes goes by the name, 'sponsored search'. Google, Microsoft and Yahoo! Offer some of the most widely used programs.

There are different models of search engine advertising. One model, known as PPC, charges the advertiser only when the user clicks on the advertisement. This model is also known as Cost per Click or CPC.

There is also a Cost per Impression or CPM model according to which advertisers pay for impressions. If you were to use this model, you could advertise any way you wanted, using text, video, audio, and map or banner advertisements.

As the owner of a small but expanding business, it would probably suit you best to opt for advertising that is based on a keyword search. You could do this by way of a search engine such as google.com. In fact, you could make use of Google's AdWords service which permits a company to link to a website, when the user looks for a keyword specified by the company. A small fee is charged for this facility.

There are several other options with search engine advertising and you would do well to do some research and identify the one that would suit you best. It could make all the difference to the responses you get from prospective clients.

29. Enter into a joint venture

This is an excellent idea, as a joint venture will give you the benefit of collective financial and other resources at your disposal. As an owner of a small business, it would really pay off to partner your company with another, as numerous examples have already proved.

And if you decide to get together with a well-known company, you will get plenty of publicity as well. It takes a great deal of time and expense to accumulate knowledge and develop products. Therefore, it's clear that small companies stand to gain significantly from partnering with larger companies, economising on both time and money, while making gains in increased productivity.

Partner with a prominent company and you immediately obtain better credibility for your own company. In terms of practicality, you have better sales, marketing and distribution facilities at hand as well.

Forming a strategic alliance with prominent companies can create barriers to competition and keep profit margins high. Once these trends have been set, they are difficult to change.

However, if you decide to enter into a joint venture, it's important to have clearly defined goals. The most cohesive relationship will be one in which both partners stand to gain from the alliance.

30. Publishing Ezines

As an individual aiming to expand your business, you are urgently in need of publicity. Ezines are just what you need. While you may have used various methods of marketing in your quest for publicity, you can now use ezines as a kind of shortcut, with very effective results.

So what is an ezine and how does it work its magic? Well, an ezine is just another name for an electronic magazine (as the name suggests). As with any other publication delivered to subscribers, there are subscribers to ezines as well who receive them by email.

Ezines are published at varying frequencies – daily, weekly, biweekly etc. or simply when the publisher has something of interest to present to subscribers. They are sent only to people who have evinced interest in them, which automatically makes up a targeted market.

You can use ezines by referring to a Directory of Ezines to identify those that resemble your offer most closely. Buy an ad in the ezine of your choice. People who read them are already interested in the product. Success cannot be very far away! Try it out. For all you know, it could provide the magic you've been waiting for.

31. Blogging works

You can use blogs to market your products. If used in the right way, blogging offers a number of advantages in promoting your products online. For one thing, it does not entail too much expenditure. Of course, it does take time to create the content that you want to include, but that is not much of a problem, particularly if you are committed to your cause. You can also assign the task of creating content to a member of your staff.

Blogs do not set a limit on the number of messages that can be sent or the number of people who can view the messages. A blog can control traffic from search engines according to terms that pertain to the content on the page concerned. Every blog has its own page, on which you can market relevant products and services for the pages concerned. This does not involve any direct expenditure.

Blogging does away with the kind of expenditure involved in conventional forms of advertising. It represents an avenue for generating income as well as keeping in touch with clients and prospective clients. People who have used blogs have found them helpful in increasing product sales by way of a product code linked to the blog.

32. Be receptive when asked for references

In the course of expanding your business, you are going to come across any number of people who may be interested in the products and services you have to offer.

You should be ready to welcome anyone who asks to use your name as a reference. Any such request represents the opportunity of a new contact for you. The more receptive you are to such queries, the better your chances of widening the range of contacts in your particular field.

Only when you are open to such requests will people be forthcoming. You never know the extent to which such external contacts can impact on your business. So do remember that if you hold back at such times, you could be passing up a great opportunity.

Remember that you are going to need to ask for references yourself. You should therefore learn to recognise the need for other people to ask you for yours. Particularly when you are looking to expand your business, it will help you to make the most of every such contact to further your own objectives. You could also treat it as a compliment to the kind of business you run.

33. Ask for referrals

When meeting new people who may be important to the efficient functioning of your business, you must make it a point to ask them for references. You may be in touch with any number of people, all of whom will have come from different sources.

They may or may not be useful to you either as clients or as contacts, who can further your business prospects in one way or another. For this reason, you must always have a point of reference; some way of checking back with other people known to the new person you have met.

In case you are not comfortable with the idea of asking for referrals face to face, there are other ways in which you can still get the job done. For example you could make out a list of people or businesses that supply complementary products or services to your own business. You can then create a system of paying referral fees for every person forwarded to you by your referral partners.

You can use tickets, coupons etc. for the referral to carry and get your referral partners to recognise them so that they can be traced back.

34. Join a Referral Group

Particularly when you are trying to expand your business, joining a referral group is a good idea. Referral groups exist for the purpose of promoting business development and providing opportunities for personal growth. Every group is made up of members of businesses that are not in competition with each other.

Referral groups provide scope for their members to exchange valuable tips and advice on how they can strengthen their own businesses. Being a part of such a group is vital to the health of your own business as it puts you in touch with others in a similar situation and offers you the opportunity to observe how other businesses work, the issues they come up against etc.

The people in the referral group also comprise a group of reliable commercial contacts from whom you may need advice or suggestions from time to time. Referral groups also offer a number of benefits to members, which therefore create a support system. It would certainly benefit you to be a part of such a group, where there is a strong sense of belonging, regular planned meetings etc.

The next time you hear about a referral group, do take the opportunity to join it. You will be surprised at how much you can learn.

35. Join an Association

Joining an association of similar professionals to yourself who also want to expand their business, can offer you a number of benefits. For one thing, you will have access to the knowledge and experience of hundreds of people, much of which may be useful to you in your business.

An association of likeminded people in a business similar to your own can offer you a great deal of support in dealing with the problems you may be facing from time to time.

You can make friends for life at such gatherings, apart from identifying contacts that will be valuable to your commercial interests. You will also be able to learn how to make your business a full time success unless you have already done so.

Apart from all this, the advantage is that you can gain a competitive edge over others in the industry and keep in touch with news, events and emerging trends in the industry.

The Association of Shareware Professionals is one organisation that operates on these lines. Launched in 1987, it is today a huge organisation with thousands of members worldwide, committed to the advancement of what is known as 'try before you buy' software. Such associations also give you a chance to learn about business strategies and techniques.

36. Join a Chamber of Commerce

This is one step you could take in furthering the prospects of your small business. Chambers of Commerce offer what they call small business toolkits, providing solutions to problems you may be having with your small business.

For example, there's a workplace-building programme that involves employees, fosters a feeling of togetherness and boosts morale. This kind of facility can help you to devise an effective programme for your small business.

There are also provisions for screening of existing and new employees to identify problems such as drug abuse and other problems related to the background of employees. All of this is in the interests of maintaining a healthy work environment.

Employers also receive guidance through this kind of toolkit on how to locate and keep good employees. This is often extremely difficult for the owner of a small business.

There is also a toolkit to help members of the Chamber with financial planning, which you are bound to find useful. You can also find out how to procure contracts from the government.

In addition, you will get acquainted with various aspects of insurance and how to handle them - knowledge that is vital to you as the owner of a small business. And then of course, there is the basic business of office management, as well as sales and marketing knowhow, all of which you can hardly do without.

37. Sponsor a local football or rugby team

Team sponsorship is one way in which you can draw attention to yourself as the owner of a small business. If your business is one that has nothing to do with sports, you may think that this kind of sponsorship does not really have a part to play in your situation.

However, it may surprise you to know that this is not necessarily the case. You should know that there are great marketing opportunities in creating links between sporting and business activities.

If you feel that this kind of tie-up enables you to focus on one of your key client groups, then it definitely does make sense. You may consider that this kind of tie-up could give your business just the kind of boost it needs, perhaps by highlighting one or more of your products. Another possibility is that it could create an opportunity for client hospitality.

Taking such factors into account, it could work out to be quite a good idea after all. And you never know where you may go from there. Attract star athletes to advertise your products, perhaps? That would give you all the publicity you need, and more! So take another look at this idea. You may just go for it, after all!

38. Location is paramount

As the owner of a small but expanding business, regardless of its nature, the question of location must be one of your highest priorities. Naturally, you need a promising product to begin with, but no one is going to know anything about it unless they know where to find it.

And so the saying goes that the most important consideration in setting up a business is location, location and location! This vital question of location is naturally linked to other factors such as population, lifestyle, traffic patterns and competition. And then again, when you are looking at the volume of traffic in the area, you must take into account both vehicular and pedestrian traffic.

Other factors you need to take into account include those that are responsible for increasing neighbourhood traffic. One of these is the presence of other retailers, who may be attracting people to the area. You also have to take into account educational, commercial and medical institutions.

Remember that if you do not choose wisely, you will have to pay dearly for an unwise decision. On the other hand, if you have made your decision after careful consideration, you will have everything to gain. So do take care and make the right choice.

39. Improving questioning abilities

The art of asking questions the right way is a skill that relatively few people have mastered. It is also one that is worth honing, as going about this process the wrong way can have far reaching results in orders being lost, people being misled and various other difficulties arising from poor communication.

It's generally been found that asking open-ended questions to determine facts is more productive than asking closed questions. You can check this out for yourself by asking friends and colleagues questions to which the answers would be either yes or no.

On the other hand, issues that concern questions of Who, What, Why, When and Where produce different results. These are open-ended questions – difficult to answer with a Yes or a No, and are useful in getting people to loosen up.

Using open questions is a comparatively rare skill in business dealings, as a result of which, there is often a financial loss. Of these, 'What' questions are regarded as posing the least threat.

Next come the 'How' questions which put the recipient under a little more pressure because they imply the questioner's need to understand. 'Why' questions should be handled carefully because they tend to probe. Handled wrongly, they can often produce a negative response.

Investing in the development of good questioning skills is vital to enhancing productivity and providing better opportunities to generate sales.

40. Handle objections with skill

In the course of running your business, you are bound to come across clients who express objections to some product or service that has not given them complete satisfaction.

The way you respond to those objections will have an important bearing on your interaction with the client who is dissatisfied thereafter. It will also affect the client's confidence in you.

So when you are faced with such a situation, you should be receptive and encourage the client to have their say. You could also avoid responding and let the moment pass. Another approach could be to avoid letting it get to you and handle the situation with humour, which will also lighten the atmosphere.

Yet another way to react to objections could be what is known as the conditional close. Here you are acknowledging the objection, but attempting to get the client to agree to accept the product if the problem is resolved.

As you come across different kinds of clients and the kind of objections they raise, you can gain considerable experience in handling them effectively. You should be able to do so without damaging your relationship. To do this successfully will call for considerable skill on your part. Do try out some of these techniques. Pacifying the offended client will be worth the trouble!

41. Arrange seminars

You can arrange seminars to publicise your small business. You can do this easily by approaching organisations that set up such events.

All you have to do is let them know that you would like to arrange a seminar. Organisations of this kind appoint coordinators who will work with you to discuss a choice of topics and speakers that would be suitable for the event.

The coordinators prepare you for the seminar by providing you with promotional literature and other material that you can pass on to your staff. They even go so far as to look after logistical arrangements, accommodation etc., if required.

You can therefore concentrate on the kind of shape you want your seminar to take, with the question of arrangements out of the way. Here is an opportunity to acquaint the general public with your small but expanding business, a golden opportunity for both publicity and the promise of valuable contacts and future prospects.

Remember that nothing works like publicity. Once people are aware of your organisation, you will have the exposure you need. So don't miss out on it – it could well be the turning point for your business.

42. Attend seminars

Attending business seminars is an excellent way to get acquainted with the issues you will face in running your business. There are organisations that hold seminars to help the owners of small businesses like yours conceptualise, launch and expand their businesses.

One such organisation is Small Business BC, which arranges different kinds of seminars to suit your particular needs, depending on the stage of development of your business. Seminars of this kind will help you to get a grip on the principles of employment law and other human resource related issues.

Seminars of this kind also shed light on how you can identify, motivate and nurture contented employees. This is vital to the health of your business and to your happiness as its owner. Such seminars also help you to assess when you can make use of the services of a contractor, thereby averting the likelihood of expensive mistakes.

As the owner of a small business, you could benefit tremendously from attending one of these seminars. That way you will be fully equipped to deal with virtually every eventuality and take steps to guard against it. So do look out for such an opportunity and make the most of it. You will be glad you did.

43. Writing 'How To' Articles

This could be yet another way to publicise your expanding business. Consider what your business is concerned with and write articles about your area of activity. Once you have done that, you need to market your article in the right kind of journal. Your objective is to reach the kind of people you hope to attract to your business.

'How To' articles tend to stimulate a great deal of interest among like-minded people. And when your subject is concerned with your business, any interest that you generate will naturally draw attention to it. Much will depend on the kind of journal you choose to submit your article to. Ideally, it should be one that deals with subjects similar to the one you are concerned with.

You should make a list of the journals that you think would be receptive to the kind of articles you plan to write. Before you send your matter, make sure you have chosen the publications wisely. Otherwise you will not get the kind of results you expect. If you need to see quick results, you need to select the kind of journal that will review and publish articles quickly. Make the right choices and you will see results.

44. Know what turns your customers on

Asking your customers is the most powerful technique for planning or improving your marketing activities. Somewhere in the customer's head or heart lies the answer to every question. You have to get this information out to profit from it. But this is not as simple as it sounds. The reason being, many customers are not aware of what they know. It takes system, method and willingness to sift through a lot of information to get a few worthwhile ideas.

To know why customers buy your product, you may have to put yourself in your customer's shoes and think hard about their dreams and aspirations and how your product is positioned to meet them.

It is important to remember that people don't buy features, they buy benefits. So it is important to have a good understanding of the kind of benefits your customers go for. What is there in your product that makes them salivate?

If you have an idea of their demographics or their psychographic profile, you can make some safe assumptions. People who come from different identifiable groups tend to behave in certain ways. For example a middle-aged family man, with two private school going children and a large mortgage, will have certain attitudes to high priced luxury goods that will be different from a vice president of a large company or a successful businessman. Besides, their values and aspirations are also different. A widow with three children, living on family allowance and part-time earnings is moved by different emotions than an air-hostess.

45. Know what turns your customers off

Every business has its share of difficult customers, those who complain loudly and make unreasonable demands. We all know the people who are put off by minor problems and refuse to listen to reason. These are people who walk away, taking their business away with them, because they could not communicate with you. Also people who are difficult to sell to because they are hard to please or don't seem to like you.

If you could make all the problematic customers happy and eager to work with you, the benefits would be tremendous. Sales would go more smoothly and there would be more sales as well. And you and your sales personnel would find the work a lot less stressful and easier.

What is the root cause of the difficulties in your firm's relationships with customers and prospects? Research has shown that in most cases, problems arise because of communication problems with individual customers or prospects. Sometimes there could have been a small incident that could have angered or upset a customer, and this has to be dealt with very carefully. But generally such incidents are easier to handle when you get the communication style right.

So, the best overall strategy for dealing with difficult customers is to focus on how to communicate with them.

46. Identify a new market:

The more routes to market you are able to tap into, the more chance you have of gaining revenue. Listing every possible sales channel may make for a healthy looking business plan, but don't spread yourself too thin. Each route to market will require expenditure, expertise and commitment. Know exactly why you are entering each route to market and what you expect from each sales channel. Many retailers never consider the possibility of mail order.

If you already hold stocks, mail order is a relatively cheap way to expand your customer base. Start off small and local and test the market. If it works, grow to regional or national level at your own pace.

The World Wide Web is another ever-growing business opportunity. Selling through the Internet can be extremely profitable. Research the web, invest in a good website and reach a global audience at the click of the mouse.

You can also pay re-sellers or lead generators to help you sell products or services to customers, for a commission. They are exposing your product or service to customers you are unlikely to come into contact with. It's a win-win situation for all. The customers get what they want, the re-seller earns the commission and you make money.

You could explore setting up a network-marketing scheme. Especially if your margins allow for the various commission structures and a multi-tiered hierarchy. Some products like perfumes, which are small and have high mark-ups, are ideally suited for this type of selling.

47. Subscribe to a Newsgroup

Newsgroups provide an online forum, collectively referred to as Usenet. Usenet's thousands of discussion forums provide a platform where people can express their opinion on the forum's specific subject areas.

Although they are similar to mailing lists, newsgroups collect messages on 'news servers' rather than via email. As with mailing list discussion groups, newsgroups can be either moderated or not moderated.

Participation in these groups can be an extremely effective way of promoting your business. To succeed, however, you need to be able to promote your expertise rather than just flaunt your products or services. Your success in a newsgroup is directly proportional to the amount of useful information you can offer. In other words, if you provide people with useful answers to their questions, they will be receptive to learning more about your products or services.

The first step to take is to find newsgroups and mailing lists that will be useful to your business. The main searchable index of the Usenet can be found at Deja news (www.dejanews.com). Besides, you can also search through newsgroups at Yahoo.

After entering keywords relevant to your business into the search engines, you'll get back a list of messages that contain those keywords, along with the name of the discussion groups where they appear most frequently.

This gives you a good indication of the groups that will be most receptive to your direct marketing efforts.

48. Create a new product or a service

There has to be some amount of secrecy in setting up a new business. The fewer the number of people who know the finer details, the more likely that your idea will not be replicated by another company.

Depending upon the nature of business you are planning to launch, you may be able to obtain anything from cash grants, tax breaks, and access to qualified staff, to financial advice and moral support. It is your duty, as the person in charge, to evaluate every option.

A search on the Internet is the best place to start. You can log on to various organizations that exist solely to support business. Some are paid services while others are free. It does not mean that the paid services are in any way superior to the free services.

So much of the setting up of a new business comes with a price. It may sound unbelievable to entrepreneurs that there are some organizations offering free services. But the real fact is such organizations get funded - generally by the Government.

While it is good to be confident and passionate about a new business; involving a third party can mean more good ideas coming in. This gives a new business a greater chance of success.

49. Offer your product at a lower price

Several researches have demonstrated that buyers are reluctant to move from their present suppliers for a price advantage of less than 10%. This is of course a general finding; decisions on some high volume purchases often turn on a fraction of a penny. The vast majority of everyday products are repeat-purchased by companies from the same two or three sources; buyers do not like changing suppliers unless they have very strong reasons.

You may be able to produce a product at a significantly lower price than your competitors' initially - when you are operating from a back room with the invoice and accounts prepared on the dining table. The costs are naturally low at this stage.

While this is a perfectly acceptable way of starting a business, the prices to customers must not be related to costs but to prices in the market.

As a small business with low overheads, you should be able to make things at a much lower cost than competitors operating from factories and big offices. But you will be unable to expand your business beyond a certain size without incurring greater expense.

There also other ways of lowering the costs of your product without feeling the heat. You can shrink the amount of the product, substitute less expensive material, remove some unimportant product features, use less expensive packing material or reduce the number of sizes and models offered, among others.

50. Offer your product at a higher price

Successful price increase can raise profits considerably. For example, if the company's profit margin is 3% of sales, a 1% price increase will increase profits by 33% if sales volume is not affected.

A major factor provoking price increases is cost inflation. Rising costs unmatched by productivity gains squeeze profit margins, forcing companies to raise prices. Another factor for price increase could be excess demand. When the company cannot supply all its customers, it can raise its prices, ration supplies to customers or both.

A high price strategy can be followed if

* Your product is unique, or well protected with patents

* The product is difficult to make or develop

* Price is not likely to be an important consideration for the customers thinking of buying your product

* You add more value added features to your product

* You have limited financial resources and are unable to raise extra money.

You have to decide whether to raise prices sharply

on a one-time basis or raise it by small amounts several times. Generally consumers prefer small price increases on a regular basis compared to sudden, sharp increases

51. Update your product

Sooner or later you will have to modify, change, improve or drop a product from your range. Before you can do that you should know which products provide the turnover and which the profit.

Answer these five questions:

1. Does the present product range need to be changed / updated?

2. Should the current market segments be changed?

3. Should the current marketing mix be changed?

4. If the product range is to be updated/changed, should this be by product modification, re-positioning, elimination, and / or introduction of a new product?

5. If new market segments and / or new products are to be introduced, should this be done ourselves or by joining with another company?

If you are in business on your own, you will have to form a committee of one! If you have responsible people working with you, use them in your deliberations. Aim to quantify the criteria you use to come to decisions, and if it is possible, adopt a formal appraisal method.

You can also stimulate sales by

- updating/modifying the product's characteristics through quality improvement

- improving the product's functional performance,

- feature improvement. adding new features that expand the product's versatility, safety or convenience, or

- style improvement that increases the product's aesthetic appeal.

52. Establish an Advisory Team to share ideas and marketing issues

Today's customers are hard to please. They are smarter, more price conscious, more demanding, less forgiving and they are approached by many competitors with equal or better offers. The challenge before you is to produce satisfied customers.

Besides, it is not sufficient to be skilful in attracting new customers, you must keep them and increase their business. Too many businesses suffer from high customer churn or loss. You can to some extent reduce the churn.

1. By defining and measuring the retention rate

2. Find out the causes of customer attrition and identify those that can be managed better.

3. You must estimate how much profit you lose, every time you lose a customer.

4. You must estimate how much it will cost to bring down the churn rate.

5. Create a mechanism by which you can always be in tune with your front-line customers

A marketing and public relations advisory team could be formed to act as a 'think tank' to share ideas and form strong bonds with the customer.

First, you need to attend to the following basics:

1. The entire business must be involved in planning and managing the customer satisfaction and retention process.

2. The customer's voice must prevail in all the business decisions

3. Create superior services, products, and experiences for the target market.

4. Organise and make available a database of information of individual customer needs, preferences, contacts, and satisfaction.

5. Make it easy for the customers to reach your business and contact the right people with their needs, perceptions and complaints

6. Run award programmes, which recognize outstanding employees.

53. Brainstorming marketing ideas

Once you are in the know of your objectives, your target audience, competitors' activities, market news; you may find it helpful to hold brainstorming sessions with your key employees or associates to develop or fine-tune your strategy or come up with new ideas that can increase the sales of your product.

A brainstorming session will help you generate a lot of ideas quickly. It is based on the premise that like-minded group of people working together with common objectives can generate a wide range of ideas than the same people working as individuals. For such sessions to be fruitful there should be no curbs on the ideas generated.

The main factor that works in favour of such sessions is the low level of inhibition and high enthusiasm within the group as compared to a more formal meeting. But one must guard against some individuals who try to be 'know all' all the time.

An experienced facilitator is a prerequisite for brainstorming sessions. His role is not to generate ideas but to assist the participants to come up with great ones.

Successful brainstorming sessions generally have about eight participants and run for a minimum of three to four hours.

54. Publish Newsletters for clients and prospects

A Newsletter is a good way of keeping in touch with your clients, prospects and the media. A good way to start off is by getting the newsletter initially designed by a professional graphic designer and subsequently producing it in-house, following the design parameters. This way you can keep the production costs low and yet have an attractive newsletter.

The newsletter keeps clients and prospects informed of new developments, new product features, new customers, special offers and so on. If you want people to preserve your newsletters, it may be a good idea to punch holes in it so that it can fit in a binder. You may also consider distributing the binder with the first issue, or better still offer it on request. Needless to add, people ordering a binder are very good prospect material.

You may also want to invite the recipients of your newsletter to reproduce articles free, provided they give acknowledgement to the source. You can request them to contact you for permission to use the article. You can then keep a file for such requests. You will immediately know which type of articles pull in the most requests and where they have been placed.

A good newsletter can help you bond with your clients, besides providing you with opportunities to get publicity.

55. Publish an article

Placing an article in an appropriate magazine is not very difficult. Even if you can't write, there are several 'ghost writers' who can help you out for a fee. Your spokesman or the Brand Manager of the product can have his or her by-line on the article. This provides them with a platform to display their grasp over the topic.

Besides, you must know the medium, the topics it covers, its readership; then crafting a story to appeal to the readers is not too difficult.

If you have an idea for an article, your best bet would be to contact the Editor by phone or email explaining the idea and requesting the name of the person to contact for further discussions. Also, get the names of personal assistants and secretaries as you speak to them. Inform them why you think the story is interesting, why the writer is special, how important it is to have the story in the publication. They can help a lot in following up and getting the story published in the magazine.

56. Develop a brochure

A brochure can be an ideal promotional tool to pre-sell your product to the target audience. It should describe the benefits of the product and create a desire to own the product.

A good brochure should:

* Get prospects excited about doing business with you

* Supply enough information to support a purchase decision

* Convey a strong positive impression of the product

* Support all your marketing functions by serving as a handout, mailing piece, giveaway at events and trade shows, among others.

It should contain technical specifications, dimensions of the product, where it is available and the price and so on. Ideally, a brochure should make it easy for a prospect to decide on the product and perhaps even recommend it to friends.

For maximum impact the brochure copy should be written with the prospect in mind. All his fears, aspirations, expectations should be addressed in the copy. The headline should highlight a key customer benefit and take a prospect through awareness, interest, desire and action stages.

To ensure that your brochure does everything it can to help you sell, you first need to analyse the possible uses of the brochure. Don't start on the brochure without a clear list of its objectives. Otherwise it won't be designed to fit those uses and you will be disappointed.

57. Take part in exhibitions /trade shows

An exhibition has several shades of hue. It can be a private reception in a local hotel room; a small 'by invitation only' show; a trade fair focused on a specific industry or a glittering international event.

The objective of participating at an exhibition is to meet as many visiting buyers as possible. When you participate in organized exhibition or trade shows, you are in competition with all similar exhibitors.

Whether or not you should exhibit will depend on the degree to which interest in your product can be stimulated and sales promoted. Except with small, low-priced goods, products are not purchased and taken away from exhibitions. Orders are often placed, but more follow-up letters or visits are necessary before an actual order is placed.

There are a number of exhibitions suitable for the small business. But you must be clear about your objectives before agreeing to participate. If you are thinking of taking space in such exhibitions, try to obtain literature and regulations as early as possible. If it has been held before, examine the statistics on attendance etc. You can also contact people who have exhibited previously and get their opinions.

Lastly, determine if the expenditure is well within the ad budget and can be justified.

58. Timely Press Releases to announce important news

Details about your product can appear in the press in two main ways: advertising and editorial mention. The difference being, you have to pay for advertising but not for editorial mention. The catch being it depends on the discretion of the editor. The vast majority of editorial content is prepared from press releases, received by the publication. The only requirement is that it must be news.

News can be of two types:

1. An event that occurs.

2. An event that is constructed arranged or contrived.

Consider the geographical area of interest that a news item might affect and the extent to which media covers that area. An item of purely local news will not interest a national newspaper. But something of interest to the whole country – even if it concerns a small locality – would be of interest to a national paper.

The press release should not be more than two or three pages of double-spaced printing, with a compelling headline and introduction, accompanied perhaps by a photo. Make sure that the photo has a caption and that the press release has a contact point-names, phone and email. Your objective is to get a story or at least a mention in the publication.

For the small business, the value of being mentioned in editorial columns of publications is continuity. It is the occasional but regular little tap of publicity that develops the image in the mind of the general public and target audience.

59. Get trained to handle media

If you are the spokesperson of your business, it will stand you in good stead to go in for media training. The training programmes last for a day or two and is designed to give you the confidence to face various kinds of interviews, e.g. a TV studio, a friendly chat, a hostile interview-among others.

These programmes help you get accustomed to cameras, flash bulbs, lights and microphones thrust under your nose, know how to control the flow of questions and answers, and enable you to communicate in a variety of situations.

A well-trained person is also trained to deflect awkward questions and bring the focus back to the core message that he is communicating.

A good training programme not only provides rehearsals for various types of interviews but also educates you on how to develop specific messages for different kinds of media. Besides, there is also role-playing, videotaped to enable the participant to figure out what aspects need to be improved. Sometimes professional journalists will be brought in as interviewers so that the scenario is as real as possible.

The focus will be on familiarisation with the message. This is to ensure that you communicate effectively, whatever the situation.

60. The power of customer testimonials

Many well-clued marketers have been using customer quotes and testimonials very effectively in direct-response print ads, brochures, and letters.

Basically, the idea is to let someone who the prospect will believe do the selling instead of you. Since you are the marketer, nobody is going to believe you when you say that you are offering a superior product.

The question is who can this someone be? It can be anyone who has a legitimate, authoritative opinion about your product, service or business. They could be your customers, friends in management positions in business, experts in your industry or technology, anyone who runs a consulting, real estate or insurance firm and so on.

You have plenty of opportunities to talk to people in most of these categories. it will be perfectly natural for you to ask them for their opinion on a specific question concerning your business. Take advantage of these opportunities to ask the question and see what raw testimonials you can get.

When you approach a well-known individual for a quote, your odds of success are a lot lower than when you approach your own customers or people whom you already know. If you keep trying, you will probably get quotes from one or two.

Many people just don't feel comfortable lending their names for such testimonials - so don't be too pushy. Besides, stay away from those who raise the question of payment for giving you the quote.

61. Test your Direct Mail list for performance

The most important element in direct mail advertising is the list of names and addresses. The kind of customers you are looking for will have a bearing on the list. If you are looking at mass mailing, the telephone directory is a good place to start. A better option would be the electoral rolls, which can be inspected at the local library.

If you want to contact buyers in factories, use the yellow pages and the various trade directories. You can also contact List brokers, who will supply you with a list as narrowly defined as you wish - but at a cost. A better option would be for you to spend a few hours in a reference library and photocopy the relevant data. This is a cost effective way to build a list for a small company.

Plan your direct mail as a campaign. Merely sending a single mailer to the target audience will not help, as people don't respond quickly. Send different mailers to different target groups and test the response. Stick to the approach that achieves the maximum response.

The list is all-important. But don't forget the relevance of the message to the target audience. If you make it easier for the addressees to reply; your response rate will automatically shoot up.

62. The importance of cash discounts

When you have made a sale and delivered the product or service, you raise an invoice. If the purchase has been made on credit, the moment the credit period (normally 30 days) is over your money is just like a free loan to the customer.

If there are delays in payments, you may have to increase your working capital to fund them. If you are borrowing money from the bank, you have to pay the bank interest. This is another cost that which you have to include in the price.

Cash discounts are generally offered for early payment. For example "2/10, net 30" means that payment is due in 30 days and that the buyer can deduct 2% by paying within 10 days.

All your invoices and price sheets should include a percentage on cost to cover the normal credit you grant. This is generally one month after the receipt of the invoice.

Allowing slow-paying customers their own time to settle the invoices means the same as cutting your prices. If you are dependent on such customers for your sales, remember to include a good margin for this in your price.

Make sure you issue outstanding statements to customers indicating the invoices and the amounts due. Follow it up with telephone calls to ensure that immediate action is taken

63. Give your regular clients a discount

Many companies will adjust their list prices and give discounts for early payment, volume purchases and off-season buying. Companies must tread carefully or they will find that their profits are much less than planned.

Research findings clearly show that in most product categories buyers are not too price-sensitive. They are willing to pay a higher price for better features, customer service, quality, added convenience, and the brand name. Thus it may not be a good idea to plunge into price discounting to respond to low-price attacks.

Salespeople in particular are quick to give discounts in order to close a sale, but the word gets around that the company's list price is "soft", and discounting becomes the norm. Besides, these discounts also undermine the value perception of the offering.

You can use discount as a useful tool to bond with your regular customers and also gain some concessions in return:

1.   You can offer an attractive discount if the customer is willing to sign a three year contract.

2.   If the customer is willing to order electronically, thus saving your company money.

3.   If the customer agrees to buy in truckload quantities. It can be either be cumulative (which encourages

buyers to concentrate purchases of a product with one supplier - as the total of purchases increases during the year the discount increases) or non-cumulative (that applies to any one order and is determined by the size of the order). The purpose is to encourage buyers to place larger orders and enjoy a lower unit price. A small business can profitably use this type of discount.

64. Make your business card work for you

Your business card is often the first contact someone has with you or your business. Sometimes it is the only marketing communication a prospect has. Therefore it is a good idea to make sure that your business card follows the rules of good marketing communication by building both emotional and rational involvement. This means that it needs to communicate the information a prospect needs to figure out what you have and how to contact you easily when he needs it. That's the rational involvement goal.

Do remember that the card also has to appeal to prospects on a basic emotional level too. Imagine a prospect looking through a pile of cards including those of your competitors. Why would the prospect pick yours? What makes it call out to people?

Basically, you have to ensure that your card makes a powerful, positive, personal impression. Most cards don't. They are dull. Even those that are clean and professional generally emphasise the information but fail to make an impression.

To make a personal, powerful, positive impression, you don't have to do anything outlandish and make a negative statement. All you have to do is strive for a sophisticated, professional image – with better quality paper, a more beautiful logo, an unusual vertical design, or an attractive use of colour. More importantly, focus on a well-presented company name and logo.

65. Read marketing books, market research studies and record your ideas

You may often attend marketing seminars, read marketing books or market surveys pertaining to your product or industry. Many a time you get wonderful ideas. Get into the habit of recording them. They may prove to be more valuable than you think. The important point is to gain exposure to various activities that stimulate creative thinking.

By merely making notes or recording your ideas, you stimulate their production and soon generate many more. You could perhaps keep a large daily planning book, with space in it to write down the appointments for the day and also the ideas that come up. Then, you can flip through the pages when you are stuck and pick a good idea to follow through.

You can also keep 'idea boxes' where you can toss your own notes or interesting articles that stimulate your thinking. You can also keep a miniature tape recorder in your briefcase and dictate ideas into it. You can get the tapes transcribed so that you can read them later.

You need to come up with your own system for recording ideas. Whatever works best for you is the right one, so try several.

66. Get a Freephone number

Since telephonic communication is so widely used in commercial dealings all over the world, providing your clients with a Freephone number where they can contact you is a wise move.

The Freephone number will allow you to pay for incoming calls, so the customer does not incur any expense. As a result, the availability of a Freephone number encourages customers to call with their queries etc. In the process, contact with clients is strengthened.

Although the actual expense of calling a company is not so steep, the availability of a Freephone option also has a psychological effect on the customer. Many companies still use customer support lines with calls costing £1 a minute.

Although the company may generate a substantial amount of income from such a move, it is not customer friendly. In fact, once a customer realises how much he is being charged, it's quite likely he will move on to another supplier.

Freephone numbers tell customers you care about their convenience. It also suggests that the company is financially sound enough to be able to offer such facilities. So do consider using Freephone numbers to boost the image of your business and preserve customer loyalty.

67. Use Advocacy to advantage

You may benefit from the practice of using advocacy to promote your small business. Advocacy campaigns depend on planning and analysis and forging bonds with citizen groups. Advocates may consist of formal or informal groups that work to achieve certain objectives.

For instance, advocates lobbying against the use of tobacco believe that stringent policies are required to implement effective control. Liaisons with advocates for the promotion of small businesses can assist your company to achieve its target. Such advocates arrange meetings with state agencies in the interest of promoting development.

Advocacy groups work in partnership with regional forums that get together to review business policies and plans. This includes briefings and technical information about permitted limits for projects in metropolitan areas. If you are looking to expand your small business, you would do well to get in touch with one such group.

That way you will know you have the backing of an established group, which can help you to achieve your goals. Some of the services available within the scope of business advocacy include opportunities to learn about business strategies. You could also have your plans reviewed from time to time to determine whether a particular project is feasible or not.

68. Offer discount cards

Discounts are always welcome in any area of business. You could popularise your expanding business by offering discounts on your products and services. Small businesses are known for making their offers affordable and therefore popular.

If you are offering a product or service at a discount, you can be sure that there will be plenty of takers. A customer with a discount card in his pocket has a feeling of reassurance. It demonstrates your commitment to him. It is an affirmation of your loyalty and a reminder that he stands to gain with every purchase he makes.

SmartLoyalty AG is one company that offers such cards for the convenience of clients, many of whom patronise small businesses. This is considered an innovative marketing system, offering simplicity, flexibility and economy. Customers who are offered such cards have every reason to stay on with you because they know that they stand to gain from the relationship.

So do consider offering your clients discount cards for their purchases. Whatever you may lose in monetary terms will be more than made up by the volume of clients you will gain once word gets around – to say nothing of the goodwill you will generate in the process.

69. Use Direct Mail

Using Direct Mail offers you a marketing tool that allows you to adopt a focussed approach. The result is that you can target only those clients who you feel will respond.

You can personalise your message so that every person you send your mailings to is addressed directly. Organise your operations so that the mailings reach your clients precisely at the most opportune time. By sending your mailings only to people who are likely to be interested, you can make your plan cost-effective.

Even if you have financial problems you can split up your mailings into manageable sections and send them according to your convenience. Direct mail also offers flexibility so that you can use brochures, inserts, mailers etc. in place of the conventional sales letter.

Even so, it would be wise to test the market by using a limited mailing before you go the whole way. Concentrate on developing the kind of mailing list that will come as close as possible to your target market. You can try out artwork and slogans of different kinds and check back on the kind of responses you get from clients.

Direct mail is ideal for attracting the attention of new customers. However, you can also use it to keep existing customers up to date about products and services on offer.

70. Get yourself a mentor

You may have been running your business for a while and have accumulated a fair amount of experience in the process. You may also have gained considerable knowledge from the support and suggestions of family and friends.

However, as the owner of a business, it is absolutely vital that you maintain contact with a mentor. This is because a mentor is someone in the same kind of commercial environment as you, with one important difference. He has more experience than you.

Mentors often offer their services free of charge, usually for reasons of their own. For example, they may be aiming to develop their skills as consultants and teachers. And then again, no matter how much you may welcome the idea of having a mentor to guide you in decision-making etc., don't make the mistake of thinking that this is a one-sided relationship.

Remember that while you are capitalising on his knowledge and experience, he is also drawing on yours and picking up ideas from you. But when all is said and done, you definitely stand to gain much more than he does, simply because he has that much more experience. After all, he has been through it all before.

71. Learn to 'productise'

When you 'productise' your services, you are offering products in the physical sense. What you are doing is making the components of your service more accessible by delivering them in packages.

For instance, you may have great skills in playing the piano, but your market is very limited. But if you were to package your skills in the form of piano lessons for beginners in a CD, then you would be tapping into a wider market. By productising, you are making a more effective use of your skill set and making it more accessible to many more customers. Once the service has been offered as a product, it is easier for your client to arrive at a decision.

Unlike goods, services do not have fixed prices as they depend on other factors such as timing, quality, experience etc. Productising your services gives the customer a standardised, consistent, product package and a sense of control, which enables him to make up his mind. The quality never varies. Besides, you can also enumerate the benefits of the product and gain considerable credibility. This is because you can back up your claims by depending on the feedback of clients who have used such products.

So do remember that productising your services offers you considerable scope for market expansion. Go ahead and try your luck!!

72. Identify your market

In order to make a success of your business, one of the most important issues you need to confront is that of identifying your market. You need to be clear about who your target audience are. Once you have done that, you can concentrate on finding out what they need and offering them products and services that are useful to them.

You may consider identifying individuals or other businesses. Dealing with individuals is a more difficult proposition because there can be no hard and fast rules. Every individual is different and they usually have smaller budgets. Apart from that, in addressing the needs of individuals, you will be faced with the inevitable question of variation. For example, people may have different preferences that keep changing with advancing age.

Businesses are more predictable and have larger budgets to allocate to acquiring what they need. Depending on what suits you as a supplier, you may even decide to target both businesses and individuals. In such a case, you would need to look at the requirements of individual customers.

In addressing the needs of businesses, you would probably be able to offer a more limited range of products. Individuals could be offered customised products.

73. Examining other markets

In furthering prospects for your business, it is worth looking at other markets to get a general idea of market trends within your field of activity. Studying other markets will give you a basis for comparison. This will serve to give you an objective view and open your eyes to possible deficiencies in your approach and how you can address them.

The value of observing other markets also lies in being able to appreciate different market conditions, as well as the kind of incentives being offered to customers. This may serve as a creative process for you as you begin to explore new ways to tap your own market, deriving new ideas from wider exposure.

Often, such new ideas can be the springboard for a whole new phase of marketing activity. In many cases, the new ideas can become a focus for new prospects, as with companies that have chosen to diversify from their original field of activity.

Observe client responses in these markets and compare them with the feedback that you get from your own clients. The comparison could once again give you quite a few ideas on how to improve your prospects. Whatever happens, this can only be a positive experience.

74. Use webinars

You could conduct webinars, which as the name suggests, are seminars conducted over the Internet. This is somewhat like web conferencing but is different from webcasting, where transmission of information is one way only.

A webinar can be considered a live event because it is conducted according to an agenda within a definite time frame. It is also a two-way communication between the presenter and his audience.

In conducting a webinar, the presenter is able to speak over a conventional telephone connection and comment on the information appearing on a screen. Members of the audience are able to convey their responses over their individual telephones. Speakerphones are best suited for this purpose.

Webinars have become increasingly prevalent in the current commercial environment for the purpose of generating sales and conducting corporate meetings. They represent a cost effective mode of communication and a convenient method of communicating with an audience, rather than ensuring that members are all assembled together at the same location.

Although webinars were originally used for communication between high profile marketers, they are now being increasingly employed by different categories of users. Webinars also offer the additional benefit of saving people the trouble of traveling to a particular location. So go ahead and use webinars to advantage as they represent a highly effective marketing tool.

75. Try Cross Selling

Since you are trying to expand your business, you could experiment with cross selling, which may be just what you need. Cross selling is the practice of introducing new products to your existing customers, on the basis of their receptiveness to your products in the past.

The idea of cross selling is to intensify the dependence of the customer on your company, so that he is dissuaded from moving on to deal with one of your competitors.

Cross selling is regarded as an efficient way of expanding revenue, since the process of attracting new customers is becoming increasingly difficult. The best way to cross sell is to identify your client's requirements and customise your products to meet those requirements.

To maximise the likelihood of success in your endeavour and take advantage of the benefits of cross selling, there are a few considerations that you should bear in mind.

You should identify the main segments sectors that your customers fall into, and look at the products that would be best suited to each of these segments sectors. Also take into account how likely a particular customer is to buy a particular product.

Approach your client at an opportune time and you will have a better chance of success. You also need to look at the best price that you can offer. This again depends on the customer's spending power.

76. Update yourself with current marketing data

Marketing strategies for small business are constantly changing, especially as a result of new technologies, methods and tools that are created and discovered almost daily. This means you need to be up to date with the latest marketing trends if you are serious about growing your business.

Subscribing to marketing newsletters - especially those that address small businesses, therefore makes a lot of sense. Many such newsletters are free, informative and risk free. You just have to enter your email address to subscribe. You may unsubscribe at any time if you do not find the newsletter useful.

Besides, you could also read the trade journals of your industry and even of other industries relevant to your clients. You could also visit the local business library and read the current marketing journals and books.

Many a time you will receive journals free. Instead of throwing them away without opening them, it may be a good idea to glance through them. Who knows? Your next million-dollar idea may come from one of these journals.

77. Write a column for the trade press

Make it a point of knowing the editors of trade journals in your industry. You can then suggest articles for their publication. It does not matter if you can't write. You can always hire a writer to do the job for you. But what is important is your name on the by-line of a story relevant to your business.

If you contribute articles regularly, you will soon be acknowledged as an expert in your field. You can also use the reprints of the articles for self-promotion. This not only helps to build your credibility, but can also lead to more business.

Soon the media will turn to you whenever they need an opinion or a comment on your industry. One way to become an authority is to write a book on that subject. Being an author of an appropriate book confers a mantle of expertise on you.

Now, enjoy the limelight.

78. Traditional Promotional Strategies

Here are some effective ways of promoting your product or service.

- Include Your URL on Stationery, Cards, and Literature.

  This is important but often overlooked. Make sure that all reprints of cards, stationery, brochures and literature contain your company's URL. And see that your printer gets the URL syntax correct. In print, you could delete the http:// part and include only the www.domain.com portion.

- Promote using traditional media.

  Don't discontinue print advertising you've found effective. But be sure to include your URL in any display or classified ads you purchase in trade journals, newspapers, etc. View your website as an information adjunct to the ad. Use a two-step approach.

  (i) Capture the readers' attention with the ad

  (ii) Then refer them to a URL where they can obtain additional information and perhaps place an order.

- Develop a Free Service.

  It's less effective to invite people with a message, 'Come to our site and learn about our business.' It's quite another to say, 'Use the free kitchen remodeling calculator available exclusively on our site.' Make no mistake, it's expensive in time and energy to develop free resources such as this, but it is very rewarding in increased traffic to your site. Make sure that your free service is closely related to what you are selling so the visitors you attract will be good prospects for your business.

- Issue News Releases

   Find newsworthy events (such as launching your free service) and send news releases to print and Web periodicals in your industry. However, opening or redesigning a website is seldom newsworthy these days. You may want to use a Web news release service or place your website URL in online copies of your press release to increase popularity.

79. Email Strategies

Don't neglect e-mail as an important way to bring people to your website. Just don't spam. That is, don't send bulk unsolicited e-mails without permission to people who you have no relationship with.

Mailing lists can be segmented into:

Opt In Marketing: This is when the target audience specifically tells you that he or she wants to get the specific e-mails that you tell them you are going to send.

Opt Out Marketing: This means that you can e-mail someone blind one time. Within that message, you plainly tell the recipients that if they don't want to receive future e-mailings, they should opt out and remove their name from the list. You must give them an easy process to remove their details from the list.

E-mail is increasingly seen as the ultimate direct marketing tool that can achieve the kind of response only dreamt of in the days of traditional forms of direct marketing. Its many advantages include:

- Cost: is inexpensive vis a vis traditional methods such as posting mail shots or cold calling.

- Immediacy: Can be sent and received in seconds. Thus provides instant results.

- IEvaluation: Due to the self-documenting nature of the Internet, the results can be measured by the number of recipients who opened the message, clicked through to the web, made a transaction or forwarded the message to a friend.

• Availability: E-mail messages can be sent out or received at any time of the day or year.

• Environmentally Friendly: As the public at large views business attitudes towards the environment as increasingly significant, e-mail marketing can enhance your status as an environmental friendly company. After all the only resource that the e-mail uses is electricity.

• Response: Surveys have found that e-mail marketing campaigns can be as much as ten times more likely to generate a response as their direct mail counterparts

80. Create a signature file for your emails

Install a "Signature" in your E-Mail Program to help potential customers get in touch with you. Most e-mail programs such as AOL, Netscape, and Outlook allow you to designate a "signature" to appear at the end of each message you send. Limit it to 6 to 8 lines: Company name, address, phone number, URL, e-mail address, and a one-phrase description of your unique business offering. Look for examples on e-mail messages sent to you.

81. Strategies to increase online sales

Send Offers to your Visitors and Customers. Your own list of customers and site visitors who have given you permission to contact them will be your most productive list. Send offers, coupon specials, product updates, etc. Personalizing the subject line and the message will increase the response rate.

Offering freebies is a great way to generate interest in your site. Just follow these simple guidelines:

- All giveaways should in some way relate to or symbolise your company.

- If you are offering something for free online, it needs to be something you're proud of. Remember, your objective is to entice the surfer to come back and become a buyer.

Another great traffic builder for your website is online discounts. But keep the following pointers in mind:

- To have the desired effect, discounts must be perceived as valuable. You can't offer a meaningless discount and expect anyone to care.

- Also online discounts should be available only online. You want to make the surfers feel special when they're doing business with your website. This relationship entices them to buy more readily through your website and gives you some great feedback on your web marketing strategy.

82. Use Viral Marketing Techniques

With the advent of the Internet, conveying messages to a large group of consumers has become economic and fast. What is referred to as word of mouth publicity off the Internet is known as viral marketing in Internet jargon. Viral, because the message, like a virus, spreads across the network rapidly and reaches a large audience in a short period.

An effective viral marketing strategy comprises of one or more of these elements-

Gives away products or services

- Provides for effortless transfer of information

- Scales easily from small to very large

- Exploits common motivations and behavior

- Utilizes existing communication networks

- Takes advantage of others' resources

Here are some ways you can profit from viral marketing

- Create an e-mail service: An e-mail service allows you to give away free mailboxes. Every mail from that mailbox will contain a link to your site and can result in additional traffic

- E-books: If you can create a good and interesting e-book (ask one of your advertisers to sponsor the e-book - Healthcare, How to choose the right wine, etc) and give it away for free, people will want to download it, pass it on to their friends and add it to their websites for others to download

- Create a freeware program: Create a freeware program and give it away on your website. Links to your website in the program generates traffic

- Write Articles: Write interesting articles and post them on the web, allow other sites and ezines to post them and encourage their readers to forward it to their friends.

83. Post Card Marketing

Here is another effective way of marketing your product. Some important points to remember: Always use postcards that are full color on BOTH sides! Studies have shown that 83% of the general public read their mail with the address facing up. If your postcard isn't full color on the front and back, you may be missing out on the opportunity to grab your customer's attention effectively. Besides, post card marketing enjoys tremendous advantages:

1. Postcard marketing is affordable, even for the smallest of businesses.

2. When you're marketing with postcards, your competition doesn't know it. But they'll sure know it if you're advertising in the newspaper!

3. It's easy to track your results. Your card can tell recipients to bring it into your store for a special discount. Or it can ask them to use a special ordering code when purchasing from your website.

4. Postcards are versatile. In a single mailing, you can seek business from prospective customers and solicit repeat business from existing customers. Better still a postcard isn't just something to send through the mail. You can use postcards as oversized business cards; hang tags for your products and mini-information sheets.

5. Your postcards can 'brand' you and your business in ways that most marketing materials cannot. If you start and stick to a regular postcard-mailing program, you and your business will gain quite a reputation.

6. Testing an offer with postcards is easy. Just send your card to a small group of people and see how many of them respond. If you're satisfied with the results, then roll out on a bigger scale!

7. Postcards don't waste people's time - they don't even have to open an envelope to read your message.

8. Postcards don't take up a lot of space. Your customers can carry them in their pockets, or carry them in their pocketbooks, for that matter.

9. Postcards are inexpensive to print.

10. Postcards are cheap to redeem. Better yet, they have no cost until your customers redeem them.

Use the cards as marketing tools to grow your business and to market your offers offline.

84. Send out well-designed Flyers

Flyers: Well-crafted flyers can be an effective marketing tool for businesses, such as yours. While most flyers get thrown away -- often because of poor design and uninspiring copy -- your flyer can be effective simply by communicating to the advertisers the special offers. Here are five tips to help you convey a level of quality that will prompt phone calls when prospective customers find your flier on their doormats:

1. To indicate that your price quote is specific to the prospect, include his address on the flier.

2. To suggest you do quality work, print your flyer on thick paper.

3. Keep your flyer specific to the service you want to sell

4. Include some form of endorsement or testimonial on your flier. You might include a quote from a customer. With your customer's consent, include the address and the customer's name. If you work with a number of customers in the local area, you can urge your prospect to 'check our work' and list local addresses.

5. To tell more about what you do, provide a website where someone interested in what you do can learn more. Have a collection of photos and testimonials there.

In today's worrisome economy, people are less apt to part with their discretionary pounds. Taking the time to produce a flyer that makes what you do look like a good deal is worth the effort.

85. Affiliate Marketing Programme

Provides a powerful way to add profits to your bottom line -- and that's through actively participating in the 'right' affiliate program. That is, an affiliate program that's right for you.

An affiliate program is a 'no-risk' partnership that allows you to promote another company's product or service on your website to earn a percentage of the sales. As one of the company's "affiliates" (promotion partners) you earn a commission each time someone you've referred to their web site makes a purchase. You might post a banner on your web site that links to the affiliate program's site, or you might publish an article about the company and their products in your newsletter.

No matter how you promote them, it's a win-win arrangement for both parties because:

- The affiliate program gets 'no-risk' advertising. (In most cases, they don't pay you unless one of your referred visitors makes a purchase.)

- And you, the affiliate, get the opportunity to earn easy extra income without the hassle of production, packaging, shipping or customer service. Generally, there is no fee for you to join and you can leave the program whenever you choose.

So to help you choose the 'right' affiliate program, here is a list of the seven critical questions you MUST ask to ensure you make the best choice and give yourself the greatest opportunity for success.

1. Is the product or service offered for resale by the affiliate program something you would use and personally recommend?

2. Does the affiliate product you are considering promoting 'fit' with your website's theme?

3. Is the company reputable?

4. Do they stand behind their product with a solid guarantee and excellent after-sales service?

5. How good a job does the company's website do of selling their product?

6. How are commissions paid?

7. What advertising and promotional tools do they provide you with?

86. Pricing Considerations

In a competitive business environment, where there is a proliferation of brands in several categories, pricing becomes a key issue and finding the right price point is an extensive exercise involving critical thinking and strategizing.

The business objectives of your company will play a vital role in its pricing policies. There are several approaches to arrive at a price for your products.

1. Based on costs:

This approach starts with the cost structure involved in manufacturing and selling the product, such as:

- raw material costs,
- production costs,
- selling and distribution costs

You can then factor in the profit margin or ROI that you would like, in order to arrive at a final price. ROI stands for Return on Investment and refers to the level of profit that can be generated from a business in comparison to the investments and money spent on producing the product and making it available to consumers.

2. Competitive pricing:

In this approach you have to takes into account the price at which competitive brands are selling and decide on where you want to position your products. You have the following options:

- Parity in pricing: You price your products at the same level as a key competitor and compete with a similar product offering.

- Pricing below the competition: This is a competitive strategy used to achieve sales volume and market penetration quickly by offering a price advantage.

- Pricing above competition: If you believe that you have a better-quality product compared to the competition; that the consumer will perceive it to be superior and will be willing to pay more; then pricing above the competition can lend a certain premium image for your product.

3. Market demand and price sensitivity issues:

This approach is rooted in concepts of economics where alternative price points are evaluated in terms of their impact on consumer demand (called the price elasticity of demand). Also the price sensitivity within the category is studied. Price sensitive consumers typically go for low-cost products that are of reasonably good quality rather than spend more on high-profile, costlier, image driven brands. This is especially true of regularly purchased household items.

The more distinctive or unique a product is in its features

or functions, the less price sensitive consumers are likely to be. They will be willing to pay more for such products and higher profitability can be achieved.

87. Selecting hot new products to maximize your profits

In today's world of global markets and e-commerce, no business can survive if its products and / or services are not in demand. For your business to grow, you must make sure that you select hot products for maximum profits. Successful business planning involves keys to identifying hot selling items, locating potential markets, judging competitors and evaluating the real demand for products and / or services.

Product selection is the critical first step in selling that you must take after hours of consideration. Take a look around in the local market, drive round local industrial estates and shopping centres. If you're planning to go online, visit sites like eBay.com and find out what are the hot selling items on their list.

Next, you need to identify your competitors and evaluate their strengths and weaknesses. You need to establish exactly who your competition is, and their strengths and weaknesses. Consult the yellow pages, search the Internet, read local newspapers for discount offers and visit local industrial estates and shopping centers to find out who else is operating in your business sector.

This will give you a chance to study the different methods adopted by your rivals to maximize sales revenues. Try to establish your unique selling point based on these lines and find out better ways of retaining customer loyalty.

Here is a checklist that can help you find the best products that maximize your profits

1. What is the greatest benefit that the product offers?

2. How many competitors does the product have?

3. How wide is the product's appeal – both in the local and in the international market?

4. How much will be the promotion cost?

5. What exactly will be the profit margin?

6. Does the product require some support or is it a stand-alone item?

7. If you're not the manufacturer, can you ensure a steady supply of the product?

8. How much are the additional costs of transportation, inventory etc?

9. How much potential does the product have for repeat purchase?

10. Will you enjoy selling such a product?

88. Branding guidelines to grow your business

Begin by writing a mission statement. This should include your business's key features and characteristics, your advantages and anything else that sets you apart from your rivals. Try to focus on the benefits that are likely to be most relevant to your target customers at large.

Once you're over with your mission statement, you can start thinking about creating a brand that not only supports your claims but reinforces your mission as well.

Four simple steps to develop a successful product branding strategy:

- Describe the benefits of your product rather than the features

- Identify your niche target market segment sector?

- Describe the key elements that give you an edge over your rivals and

- Create tag lines that echo your mission statement successfully.

Creating a tag line is easier said than done. You can hire a professional copywriter to create an attention-grabbing tag line for you, but be prepared to spend quite a large sum. If you're limited by your budget, you can study the commercials of successful brands and try to grab ideas and concepts.

With the recent boom in online trading, Internet branding is what more and more new entrepreneurs are interested in. Here, your approach to product branding is different from a brick and mortar business. The Internet has a plethora of tools for effective branding and marketing through which you can transmit your own personality and identity to create trust.

You must try to establish your credibility at the very beginning as here your customers are neither able to see you nor your products. Remember; trust sells and the faster you're able to establish your credibility, the higher your sales will be.

Here are some important branding guidelines for online branding:

1. Buy your own domain name

2. Provide contact information like phone numbers, business and personal mailing addresses

3. Provide an 'About Us' page containing the owner details

4. Provide details of guarantees, if any

5. Provide secured payment gateways

6. Do not resort to Spam – be specific about your code of ethics.

Whichever way you choose to brand your business, do it with style, sophistication, and in a manner unique to your business.

89. Tips for launching a word of mouth campaign

Word of mouth advertising is simple; a person is exposed to your advertising message in a format that motivates them to tell another person.

There are some points that you need to keep in mind before you launch a word of mouth campaign:

* Tailor your advertising message for one specific audience; you cannot be all things to all people.

* Design all the aspects of your campaign with a consistent theme; use the same slogan, colors, and typeface in all of your materials

* Cover all the bases required to present a complete picture to your audience. If a person receives an email with a discount code to be used for a purchase, ensure that your order form has a space for the code to be inserted and calculates the discount accordingly.

* Test all the components of your campaign and correct any problems before you launch it to the public. If you direct your prospective customers to a landing page that generates a 'page not found error' you risk losing a sale.

* Make sure you can deliver on whatever you offer in your promotions. One unsatisfied customer could ruin your business.

* Create a feedback or suggestion section on your order form. This is a great way to find out what is on your customers' minds. Knowing which features they want helps you to improve your product or service. Give your customers a space for referrals or link your form to a 'tell a friend' form.

* Once your advertising campaign begins to generate results, follow through and send a customer satisfaction survey. This gives you the opportunity to introduce other products or services that they may need.

* Make your customers website experience as enjoyable as possible. Create your own customers' forum for your visitors to share their ideas and information with others who have used your product. Combining word of mouth advertising with other methods is a surefire way to increase your sales.

90. Web Casts to reach business-to-business audience

B-to-B marketers still look at the webcast as a 60-minute live event, completely ignoring reality. The overwhelming majority of your prospects are not likely to be available to attend your webcast at the precise hour you've selected. It's the way you present the webcast to people who visit it on another day - say, two months after the live even - that will have the most impact on lead generation. The first step: don't think of the webcast as a one-hour event. Think of it as a three-month campaign.

That means making the post-production webcast the best it can be for that format. First, remove the obvious items, such as instructions for posting questions and taking instant polls (which will no longer be relevant after the live event is over). Second, edit the material so that it is as compelling and brief as possible. Third, create a layout that allows for attendees to get in and out of the webcast in as little time as possible.

Webcast attendees in the B-to-B space want information in as little time as possible. Give them quality data that they need and can't get elsewhere and you'll win them over. But the first part of that battle is convincing them that you do indeed have that quality data. The best way to convince them is to show them as quickly and cleanly as possible.

Don't limit your webcast imagination. Most B-to-B marketers live by their customer profiles, focus group data and whatever insights into their prospects they can obtain. Yet they leave a diamond mine like a webcast virtually untouched.

The webcast can be a wonderfully powerful marketing tool. Contact your target advertisers and 'sell them' the idea of a web conference to your audience on a topic that is relevant to both.

91. Turning customers to friends

Forming long lasting friendships is not easy. When we are young, we usually have a lot of friends, but as we grow older and settle into life, most find their friend's circle narrowing and growing tighter to include a few very close friends.

Your list of acquaintances is often much larger than your list of genuine friends.

It could be worth your while to bond with a few of your customers and try to genuinely help them and be their friend in their hour of need. It is thus imperative that you work at the friendships that you have and retain the good association with the friends that you have.

People are generally drawn to those who make them feel good about themselves. Critical, overbearing people who don't show adequate sensitivity towards other's feelings often have a tough time maintaining friendships.

Once you make a friend, you have to work towards maintaining that friendship and it's really quite simple and instinctive. The following six simple insights into maintaining friendships will ensure that you keep your friends beside you and bask in their friendship for a long time to come.

Six simple insights into keeping friends:

   1.   Be supportive

2. Listen

3. Be easy going and uncomplicated

4. Nurture the friendship

5. You have to be fun to be with

6. Don't be demanding

92. Dealing with Stress

Your mental fortitude comes into play in dealing with stress. An executive fighting against all odds to meet a delivery deadline to an important client could get as stressed out as a homemaker planning a huge dinner party. A teen facing a major exam could likewise be as stressed out as a boxer preparing for an imminent boxing bout with a formidable opponent.

Stress is a state where you strain your nervous system with worries and negative thoughts. You dwell for a prolonged period of time on worries regarding bad outcomes instead of looking for solutions to the problem. You may dwell on the past and not move ahead in thought and spirit. This stretches your ability to handle your emotions to maximum limits and when you can no longer endure the tension, it begins to manifest itself in stress related problems and behavior like outbursts, headaches, irritability, eating too little or too much and so on.

These behaviors attributed as stress symptoms are a signal that you need to take corrective action and improve your state of mind. To deal with stress, there are many simple techniques that you can use.

1. Problem-solution mode

2. Positive thinking

3. Use De-stress methods: Meditation and imagery, humor therapy, leisure activity, music therapy and exercise

93. See the brighter side

There are two sides to every coin, there is a positive and a negative, there's optimism and pessimism. And if your thinking dwells only on the negatives, it deters progress.

When anyone, a colleague, family member or friend approaches you with an issue that they are looking at only from a dark or negative side, you can steer them away from negativity by showing them the bright side of the same issue.

For instance, what would you say, if a co-worker complains that the volume of email queries and the necessary correspondence in response is taking up too much of his or her time and is a distraction throughout the day?

Firstly, you can suggest that that the email be checked at 2 or 3 specific times in a day and that there is no need to have an email alert throughout the day.

Secondly, point out how lucky we all are to be living in these times of technology development and how much more time consuming paper based communication used to be.

This process of looking to the positives in a potentially irritating or difficult situation and organizing yourself to take it in your stride is the essence of looking at the brighter side of things.

It is an approach in which you don't let yourself or those you deal with get bogged down by anything. Those who approach you with a problem should always be able to walk away with positive thoughts in their mind, because you have influenced them to see the brighter side of things. This does not mean you have to have all the answers, quite often you may not be able to come up with a concrete solution, but it is the positive approach that is a stepping-stone to eventually finding a proper solution.

94. Politeness can push up your sales

Politeness and cordial behavior is very important in all dealings, whether it's an office environment, interacting with family or friends, dealing with customers or making a bank transaction, whatever the situation, politeness goes a long way in ensuring that you create a positive feeling and more importantly get others to comply with any request that you may have.

Politeness has to come across in your wording, your tone of voice and your body language in order for it to work on the other person in a positive way. This is an important facet of spreading harmony.

Two women were out indulging in their favorite pastime – shopping. They reached the venue for a half-price sale of clothes with a lot of excitement and anticipation, hoping to find some good clothes at bargain prices. A man stood at the entrance of the shop. As the two approached the store, he told them in a rude manner to leave all the bags that they had with them on a table placed outside the door.

The store apparently had a policy of not allowing people to carry any bags inside (except for a small handbag or purse) because they had bad experiences with theft in the past. The rudeness of the person brought down the high spirits that the women had been in before they reached the store. The mood was lost. They walked around the store for a few minutes and walked away without making a single purchase.

A few days later, the women were once again on their outing and approached another store where there was a huge discount sale. There was a sign outside the door that said: "We have a small request for our esteemed patrons. May we request you to please leave all your bags in the space provided at the entrance? It will leave your hands free to do your shopping in comfort. Our security personnel will ensure the safety of your belongings. Thank you very much for your cooperation".

 The message was so politely put across with no insinuation about possible stealing, that the women did not mind obliging. They then entered the store and even made some purchases without any ill feeling.

95. Establish a reputation as being reliable

If you want to influence people and bring about positive changes in attitude and behavior, you have to first build up your credibility as a reliable person. The reliable person is someone who is highly dependable, trustworthy and a pillar of strength in times of crisis.

Firstly, you have to be approachable

Secondly, once people approach you, they have to be able to trust you enough to confide in you and take your advice.

Thirdly, it is your sound judgment and good advice that should drive people back to you again and again.

You can build such a reputation for yourself if you show consistency in your dealings and take a genuine interest in the people who interact with you.

Anyone who approaches you - customers, your employees, peers, and friends - for counsel will consciously or unconsciously ask himself or herself the following questions:

- Is this person sincere enough for me to confide in?
- Will there be any ulterior motives in the advice that I'm given?
- Can I trust this person to be loyal and keep the conversation and the problems discussed, strictly in confidence?

- Am I placing my trust in someone who will give me the wrong advice?

Your reliability can be established if you show genuine interest in helping others, avoid giving slapdash advice and instead carefully think through and give a sincere opinion. You have to make your opinion count for something and anyone who approaches you should be able to walk away with a lighter burden on their shoulders.

96. Learn to be organized

People in key positions, those who have been successful and much admired in their professions, by and large have a common thread as far as their work style goes.

They operate in an extremely organized manner. Barring some of the 'creative types' (like artists, musicians, and the like, for whom creativity stems out of turmoil and chaos) most of those who have tasted success have an extremely organized and systematic approach.

Tips on being organized:

- Carefully plan your work day and chart out the day's schedule

- Have an orderly placement of files and objects on the work desk: Everything you need has to be easy to locate and it helps to have habitual placements – For instance, appointment diary, stationery always in the same spot

- Jot down things as and when an important thought come up. Don't leave everything to memory.

- Use post-it pads to make short notes to colleagues: reminders, vital information that may be overlooked, follow ups, goodwill gestures

- Establish and maintain a regular workday pattern as far as possible

- Have a regular system of constant checks and reviews. Taking stock from time to time is important

- Make sure you have everything you need before you begin working on anything. When you have to interrupt your work to go look for a file or get some stationery, it tends to break the train of thought and vital points may be lost in the bargain. While multi-tasking is important, do one thing at a time, complete one task within a time slot before you move on to the next. If your train of thought leads to another project make a note of the idea and return to it later.

- For any assignment that you attempt, make very sure that you first understand and are very clear on the objectives. Unless you have clarity on this vital first step, your output will suffer.

- Follow procedures, follow a systematic style of work, go step by step and take no short cuts.

The discipline of being organized cannot be achieved overnight and has to be cultivated over a period. The example you set and efficiency that you bring to your work has a definite influence on those who interact with you and soon you will notice others emulating and adopting an organized approach. As they say - imitation is the best form of flattery. If you are able to influence people in your work sphere to pursue an organized approach like yours, it will show in the long run in the improved efficiency of your business.

97. Develop time management skills

An important aspect of self-improvement and greater productivity is the ability to manage your time efficiently. Not only should you follow these guidelines yourself but also inculcate them in others that you interact with in order to improve the overall effectiveness around you.

1.   Make a list of tasks, don't leave out anything, all chores however trivial take up TIME

2.   Prioritize your task, and budget an approximate time

First things first: Do first, the tasks that in your view are most important. Don't try to place the tasks that you like first, this is a usual tendency. Efficient time management requires that you deal with top priority and urgent, important tasks first.

1.   Take help: If you can take help on certain jobs, then do so. You don't have to do everything yourself. You can save yourself a lot of time by delegating within your office

2.   Concentration: Don't spend more time than necessary on any task and you can achieve this by simply concentrating. If you mind wanders, it takes more time to complete the task. Concentration is the key to complete any task within a reasonable time.

3.   Budget for relaxation time: Never overstretch yourself. Build in a few minutes of relaxation

between major tasks. It will revive you and help you to execute the next job on your agenda to full potential.

4. Review: Take stock at the end of the day and see if you were able to complete all tasks and if you were able to complete it within the budgeted time.

If you want to influence others around you to practice time management, set the example yourself and others will soon follow suit. Setting an example is one of the most effective and potent ways to bring about any change in work culture.

98. Effective Communicator

How to develop good communication skills? Here are some tips to help you along

- Proper preparation on what you plan to say at a meeting. Write it down and rehearse if required

- Being thorough in your understanding of the subject or topic of discussion

- Clear understanding of organization structure and flow of information

- Not talking down to people but making them comfortable in your presence

- Simplicity of words – there is no need for verbosity or using difficult to understand high-flown language. If people don't understand the complex words that you may be using, your communication effort is a failure, no matter how good your presentation is or how skillful an orator you are.

- The ability to listen - the art of communication requires an ability to listen too. Unless you listen, you will not have all the facts before you. Unless you know all the relevant facts, you cannot make convincing statements.

- Sport an affable manner even when faced with a difference of opinion. Divergent views are a fact of life. Not everyone can subscribe to the same views and ideas. Appreciating a different view point and accepting the relevant ideas from other's views is also important in developing good communication skills

99. Mental framework of a good leader:

These are the qualities you need to be a good leader

- Leaders have the ability to handle pressure: Display composure in tough times and courage in a crisis situation. It is this courage and composure that gives strength to others and helps in the collective handling of difficult situations

- Leaders are astute enough to seize opportunities: Enjoy challenges and never let a good business opportunity pass you by

- Leaders like to take charge: Leaders like to be in control and enjoy the responsibility that leadership places on their shoulders.

- Leaders have a winning attitude and thrive on success

- Leaders are perceptive, shrewd and are wise enough not to be misled by those with vested interests

- Leaders have a confident air about them and they believe in themselves. This confident air reassures others and inspires trust in the leader's capabilities

- Leaders are humble enough to learn from mistakes, sincerely listen to other's views and are open to ideas and suggestions

- Leaders have a self-awareness of their own strengths and weaknesses and can gauge the strengths and weaknesses of others and use this knowledge to build on the strengths of individuals by assigning them to projects suitable to their strengths

- Leaders strive for a broad understanding of all aspects of their profession, but use the advice of experts to make the right decision. How can you guide others and use your judgment if you don't know the nuts and bolts of your own profession?

- Leaders understand team dynamics and use the diversity in teams to get unusual ideas and new ways of approaching the job.

- Leaders have emotional maturity brought on by a highly developed emotional intelligence.

These leadership qualities that a good leader embodies bring out cutting-edge thinking and efficient performance in others. It is a mindset that is confident and used to being at the helm of things but humble enough to constantly learn and evolve. And it goes without saying that all leaders need a vision and it is their vision that sets the growth path and motivates people to strive towards a common goal

100. SUCCESS depends on your mental make-up

To be successful at whatever you do in life, you have to first begin by understanding yourself.

- What motivates you?

- What are your goals and objectives in life?

- Where do you see yourself 5 years from now and are you mentally prepared to take on the challenge to get there?

- What is your self-image and is this realistic enough or do you unconsciously project yourself to be better than you actually are?

- How important is it to you to excel at whatever you do? And so on.

If you are honest with yourself you will be able to find out what your real frame of mind is and then be able to gauge what you should do to work towards your goals.

If you understand the mindset of your co-workers, family and friends, you can learn to deal with them better and even influence situations in your favor.

Understanding these mind states is a first step towards overcoming the disadvantages caused by certain characteristics or conversely heightening the advantages offered by certain characteristics.

101. Carry business cards at all times

When you are trying to expand your business, you are likely to be on the lookout for contacts wherever you go. This means you need to be fully prepared to take advantage of opportunities as and when they present themselves.

It is therefore vital that you carry your business cards with you every day, because you never know when you are going to need them. Your ability to attract interest will depend largely on your own ability to engage the people you meet and hold their attention.

However, meeting people in business is all about maintaining contact and the most effective way you can do that is to offer your business card. Always make sure that you are carrying an adequate supply.

Otherwise, you may even find that at some critical juncture when you merely need to hand over your card, you are unable to do so because they have run out!! That would certainly be a pity, wouldn't it?

You could still maintain contact with the person concerned, but you would come across as rather unprofessional in such a situation. And that would never do, would it? So don't let it happen to you – your card is very important!!

102. Design a personal nametag to wear at important events

In expanding your business, you need to be aware of opportunities for publicity – publicity for your organisation and your products, as well as publicity for yourself.

It is vital for you to keep track of occasions and events where you will have an opportunity to further your cause in one way or another. And there is no reason for you to restrict yourself. So why not be a little adventurous and make your own statement?

You can do so quite easily with a personal nametag that carries your name as well as the name of your company. Use it with confidence at high profile meetings where it will be important for you to leave a lasting impression. After all, since you are running a business of your own, even if you have a reliable team backing you, the responsibility for the visibility of your business will largely be your own.

This is surely the right time to splash out a little and find a unique way to make an impact in the places that matter. You will probably be able to see this impact for yourself when the time comes. That should really make you feel good! So go for it and enjoy the show!!

103. Keep track of market trends that could affect your prospects

As an entrepreneur with the primary responsibility for the prosperity of your business, it is vital for you to keep track of trends in the market that could make a difference to your business performance.

You need to be acutely aware of market developments, pricing issues, new trends, new products that have been launched and the emergence of new competitors who may present a challenge to your organisation. Whatever happens, you need to be ready at all times to rise to the occasion.

Let's say a new product is being launched. This could be a situation that may present an opportunity for you to advance one of your own products. Or perhaps you could enter into a tie-up with another company? Once again, there is excellent scope for publicity for your company.

And then again, there is the question of fluctuating demand, which will affect the performance of your products directly. For example, you need to be sure that when demand is high for one of your products, you are adequately stocked to meet it.

You also need to be aware of falling demand, so that you are not stranded with an excess of some product that has declined in popularity. Do keep your wits about you – it will make all the difference!!

104. Keep abreast of market research findings that will be important to you

When you are running your own business, it is vital for you to be acutely aware of everything that is happening in the industry. Along with the prevailing market trends, do remember that research findings presented by market research bureaux could be very important to you.

Market research findings are derived from studies conducted in considerable detail. It is worth keeping track of them, particularly when they pertain to your product, industry or area of operation. Research findings can turn up information about your competitors or products that would present contention to your own in the market.

Such information could work to your advantage or to your detriment. Either way, you can hardly afford to be in the dark. For instance, research may have shown that some product does not have very good prospects for growth. If this is a product with which your business is concerned, you will have to take urgent steps to redeem the situation, perhaps by providing a product that offers better prospects.

Perhaps you need to turn your attention to the other contenders in the market and devise a strategy to meet challenges. But most of all, as a professional, you need to have market developments at your fingertips at all times.

105. Study literature and advertisements pertaining to products offered by competitors

Given that your business will have to hold its own in the midst of a sea of competition, one of the most effective steps you can take is to get hold of advertisements and literature concerning products offered by your competitors.

Study them carefully to see how they have been presented and observe marketing strategies that have been used to advance them. You could get several useful ideas from this kind of observation to improve the presentation of your own products – or even find elements that you would wish to avoid.

The more thorough you are in making these observations, the better you will be able to counter competition. In fact, in such matters, it would be a good idea to adopt an academic approach so that you do not leave anything to chance.

A failure to observe something of significance could have serious consequences on your prospects. Ultimately, this could have negative financial implications or impact your standing in the market.

So do make the most of any opportunities that arise to study the modus operandi of your competitors. You never know when you can use one element or the other to your advantage. The ball is in your court!

106. Attend a marketing seminar

Attending seminars on sales and marketing is another effective way to improve your marketing skills. Seminars are effective as they attempt to deliver focussed and properly structured programmes over a short period. Seminars can introduce you to a lot of current ideas, techniques, concepts etc, besides helping you to decide about their suitability in your business and make you better equipped to implement them successfully.

You would have the opportunity to learn from experienced professionals with years of business and training experience in that area, who generally conduct such seminars. You will be exposed to their in-depth understanding of tools and strategies, which would work in the real world and their insights could be invaluable in expanding your business.

Attending seminars can give you practical insights into the real world of sales and marketing techniques. It can also give you ideas to adapt and use in your business. Seminar lectures are usually backed by real case studies of well known businesses to provide a broader perspective.

Seminars also offer the opportunity to meet up with others who may be in the same business and learn from their experiences. Such sharing of experiences will help in identifying the right sales and marketing tools and strategies which could be effective in your line of business. You would also become better informed about possible risks and pitfalls while implementing various strategies.

107. Promote referrals

Referrals - information about potential customers provided by mutual acquaintances - are very effective promotional tools to build your business, especially when you are starting out. Typically, most of the initial customers of start-ups come through referrals.

Many of your potential customers would be hesitant to enter in to a transaction with an unknown start-up, if you approach them directly. Referrals can give some confidence to such potential customers about your reliability and encourage them to try out your products or services.

Your initial customers or clients, staff members and colleagues are the most suited to give you referrals as they know you and your business reasonably well and can vouch for you.

To help them identify potential customers, you should clearly explain your product or service offerings and define a potential customer. Remember that the person who is making the referral should feel confident enough to recommend your product or service to others.

Many entrepreneurs are hesitant to ask for referrals, but a pro-active approach can work wonders. While asking, you should not sound too desperate or pushy as it may discourage them from giving referrals.

You should also request your sources to get feedback

from potential customers after you have made your initial sales pitch to fine-tune your strategies. Once you close a sale originated through a referral, make sure that a note of appreciation is sent to the person who made the referral.

108. Join a professional body or association

While setting up a new business, you should try to join the local business council, trade association or professional organisation. These bodies are excellent platforms to interact with other business owners and professionals and would help you to better understand the local business environment. Local business councils also act as lobby groups to protect business interests of members.

Regularly attending the meetings of such organisations and associations can open up new business opportunities, contacts and provide information about support services, which may be required for your business. Contacts and relationships through such bodies could also result in customer referrals and business leads. Potential customers would be more receptive to referrals by business and professional associations and hence the conversion rate would be high.

Business and trade associations usually try to support start-up businesses through various promotional activities among members. They would often provide you with direct access to potential customers and other opportunities to promote your business in a very cost-effective manner. Honours and awards from professional or business associations would enhance your reputation and visibility.

Professional associations and business councils often

conduct management training and skills improvement programmes for members, which would be very helpful to you.

109. Maintain a consultant card file

Most businesses need several good quality support services to succeed. These services include accounting, tax advice, staffing, designing, advertising, marketing, legal advice etc. Access to and availability of such services can be sometimes critical for your business success.

When setting up a new business, you should have a clear idea about the various support services you may require in future. Some of these services may be required frequently while others - like advice services, would be required only periodically.

As the next step, you should do a survey of service providers in your area and collect details about each of them. For support services which are required frequently and are crucial for your business, you should ensure that you have the details of as many service providers as possible to ensure that such support is available in case of an emergency.

Professional consultants provide many of these support services. Hence it is worthwhile to create a file to organise the business cards of such consultants and service providers for easy reference.

The business cards should always be organised under different services like accounting, designing, marketing etc. Even if you do not have a number of consultants or service providers for each service, it is advisable to maintain the card file in this fashion rather than organising it in alphabetical order.

110. Analyse the fee structure

If you are in a service business, the fee structure should be properly designed and structured. A transparent and clear fee structure would find favour with potential clients. Your fee structure can also become a strategic tool to differentiate yourself from your competitors.

Service businesses offer a range of services to different market segments at different price points. Pricing could vary for different clients depending on level of services and volume. Very often, service businesses compete mostly on pricing when there is not much differentiation in services offered. Hence, you as a service provider should give considerable attention to your fee structure and design it in such a way that your potential clients will find it attractive.

Analysis of your fee structure should start with a detailed breakdown of the various services offered by you. Then you should analyse your cost structure for each of those services. The cost breakdown for each service should be prepared in detail and should consider both fixed and variable components.

After fixing the cost structure, you can add a mark up to arrive at a fee structure to be offered. Proper understanding of the cost structure will help you to be flexible in your pricing and respond to pricing strategies adopted by your competition.

111. Get feedback using postage-paid survey card

Feedback from potential customers about your products and services will help you to better understand the market and requirements of potential customers. As the potential customer base defines your future market, it is of vital importance to understand the trends.

Success of your business depends on the effectiveness of your sales and marketing campaigns and strategies. Feedback would therefore be useful in assessing the response of these strategies among prospects. It could also help you to re-design your campaigns and to re-formulate your strategies, if required.

Sending post- paid survey cards along with brochures and other sales literature to potential customers is one of the ways to get feedback about your products and services from your target customer base.

The cards should be designed well, ideally with the help of advertising professionals. The copy used should be easy to understand and questions should not be very long. You should also select the questions very carefully to get the right information.

Survey cards should always be postage-paid to en-courage prompt response from recipients. You can also consider offering free product trials or small gifts to encourage prompt feedback.

112. Prepare distinct sales literature for different market segments?

While expanding your new business, you should not make the mistake of adopting a 'one size fits all' marketing strategy especially when you are offering products and services to different market segments - like other businesses, the government and retail customers. This would result in ineffective communication and lower sales conversions.

Requirements of different market segments vary considerably and hence your marketing strategy, sales literature and other promotional tools should be different for each market segment.

To begin with, you should clearly define and demarcate the different market segments you are targeting. The next step is to understand the specific requirements of each segment and prepare brochures and other sales literature to address those requirements.

Sales literature for large and high profile customers like the government and other businesses should contain as much detail as possible, including detailed technical specifications and drawings – if any. For retail customers, sales literature should be simple and easy to comprehend without many technical terms. You can consider preparing different versions of promotional literature and get feedback from potential customers before deciding on the final designs.

Attention to detail is of high importance while designing sales literature targeted at different segments. The
focus, presentation and copy should be distinct for each
segment to create a positive response. If you are hiring
marketing or advertising consultants to prepare such
literature, make sure that they have clearly understood
the market segmentation and the specific requirements
of each segment.

113. Keep updated media lists

To ensure that your press releases and other announcements get enough visibility in the local media, you should know who the key personnel at important media outlets are and ensure that your material reach the right people. Otherwise, your releases would go unnoticed among many others.

Media lists contain the details of contacts and journalists at local newspapers, television, radio and websites carrying business news. To prepare a good media list, you should study all the local media organisations and understand their areas of focus. You should concentrate more on industry or professional publications and newspapers and magazines, which give extensive business coverage.

Media lists can be kept in alphabetical order in the form of business cards for easy reference. You may keep separate lists for trade / professional and general publications, if required. Each entry in the list should have the full postal address, contact telephone and fax numbers, email addresses of the media organisation besides the names of key personnel and their direct contact numbers, if any.

The media list should be reviewed periodically and kept updated. New publications should be added to the list without delay. You should keep scanning the local media to understand shifts in editorial focus and should give

more attention to those publications which give sufficient coverage to your line of business.

114. Build and maintain media relations

Getting coverage in the local media can give your business considerable publicity at negligible cost. But getting sufficient media coverage requires a lot of effort especially in terms of building relationships with key media personnel.

They have to be provided with sufficient information about your products and services to help them write positively. Frequent media mentions about you as a business owner would enhance your reputation and visibility, which in turn would help your business.

An editor of a newspaper or trade magazine is an important person who decides on what to publish in the newspaper or magazine. While trying to build your media contacts, you should try to impress and cultivate the editors as they are the ultimate decision makers regarding content to be published. Editors of large newspapers and trade publications may not entertain direct contact with small business owners, but you can definitely try reaching out to them through other journalists.

Taking out an editor for lunch is a good way to establish or further your relationship with a publication. Meeting over a lunch, in a relaxed atmosphere would give you an opportunity to talk about your business in detail. You would also get to understand the media's opinions and views on business trends.

While trying to create a positive impression, you should not be seen as trying to promote yourself and your business aggressively. The approach should be subtle and balanced without too many negative statements about your competitors.

115. Review the media for PR opportunities

Public relations opportunities are cost-effective tools to enhance the visibility of your business. Such opportunities can be in many forms like sponsoring an event at the local school or community centre or supporting research activities of a trade or professional organisation. Such events and projects get wide publicity and media coverage, which would benefit your business.

Association with such projects and initiatives would also enhance your profile among potential customers. Events like community meetings can also offer opportunities to display your products or give presentations about your service offerings. As you would have exclusive access to such events as the sponsor, your products and services would get much better attention from potential customers. Such events are also very useful in getting business leads and referrals from the organisers.

To seize such PR opportunities, you should consistently review the local newspapers and trade publications. Information about such events appears in the media well in advance - when the organisers start planning for it. Their organisers often use early media releases about such events as an invitation for businesses to be associated.

It may be highly time consuming to scan all the newspapers and other publications, especially when you have to attend to other issues. In such cases, you may limit your review to select publications, which are focussed on your trade or profession or give sufficient coverage to your line of business.

116. Take responsibility for your business

When you are running your own enterprise and looking to expand, you need to consider all angles of the business. Your decisions will ultimately be yours alone and whichever course you take can go either way.

You need to remember that as the owner of a business, you have to take into account the costs of all that you put into it and weigh them against the benefits. You need to function in a cost-effective way and be able to derive the maximum benefit in return.

Be focussed and remember that you could well be making decisions from which there will be no turning back. Every aspect of this business is going to be your own responsibility, from matters concerning day-to-day functions, to staff welfare, to meeting your targets. And of course, the proof of your success will be your impact in the market and your ability to draw customers.

It is vital to take the time to scrutinise every facet of your commercial practice so that you are assured of the best possible results. So the more carefully you think through every decision you take, the more likely you are to choose wisely. And the results will speak for themselves.

117. Be prepared to stand corrected

As the owner of a small but expanding business, you have taken a huge responsibility on yourself. You are going to be ultimately accountable for the success of your enterprise. It has taken you time to learn and you have accumulated plenty of experience the hard way. It hasn't been easy but you have come out on top and survived several situations that came close to turning into crises.

All of that should have given you confidence in your own abilities. But don't forget that anyone is capable of making mistakes, wrong decisions and poor judgements – and you are no exception. A member of your staff may even make you aware of this. Should this happen, you must have the humility to acknowledge that you have made a wrong choice.

Only then will you be receptive to the necessity for making a change as and when you need to. Often this may be a change that will have a critical impact on the fate of your business. So do take the trouble to pay attention to any inadequacies in your business or your style of functioning. Rectifying faults can make all the difference. It's worth bearing in mind.

118. Recommend your client for an award

Among your many clients, there will be several who probably give you more custom than others – custom that has helped you to spread the word about your business. It is worth considering how you can show your appreciation.

One of the ways in which you can do this is to put your client's name forward for an award. In doing so, you are letting your client know how valuable he is to you. At the same time, you are earning publicity for yourself in proposing such an award.

Taking a step like this can also act as an incentive to existing customers to stay with you. Providing clients with awards will introduce a touch of originality into your style of functioning and tell them that you do not take their loyalty for granted.

In fact, as news of the award gets around through your existing clients, you may even find that you are suddenly inundated with new clients. And that, after all, was the idea, wasn't it? Drawing publicity to yourself and your business and proving that you can deliver is what you need to succeed – particularly when you have to survive in the midst of competition that is getting more and more intense by the day.

119. It's all about sales pitch

Sales pitch is concerned with presentation. When you are trying to sell a product to a prospective client, your success or failure to do so depends on how you put your case across and how persuasive you can be. If you are meeting a client in person, your appearance and bearing will also play a part.

To guard against the eventuality that you may not be able to come across quite as you planned, it is worth considering practising the kind of delivery you would like to present. Even if the client is not particularly interested in your product, the way you present it can make all the difference, to the point of making him change his mind.

Take care not to sound too stiff. You can plan how to present whatever you want to say, but make sure you do not take too long to get to the point and arouse interest in your product or service. Once the client's curiosity has been aroused, you could say half the battle has been won.

When you have reached this point, you can even proceed to start building a rapport with the client. It is vital to your success to be as natural as you can. Try it and watch the results!!

120. Get a handle on copywriting

If you can learn copywriting, you can really be in control of your business prospects. Copywriting is all about publicity and how you can project yourself.

Learn to do it yourself and you will have the tricks of the trade right in the palm of your hand. It's a fact that it would also be more economical than hiring someone to do it for you, but that's a side benefit.

The main advantage for you will be to learn how to give your copy the slant that you want to achieve the desired effect. You know what your business involves and your reasons for projecting yourself in one way or another. You also know what you stand to gain if you do it right and what you can lose if you don't.

Your business is close to your heart and it is worth doing whatever you need to make it a success. Your success will affect more than just you alone. It will affect your business and everyone who is involved with it. And most of all, it will affect your reputation in the market. Surely that bears thinking about. Of course it does. So go for it! You have nothing to lose and everything to gain!

121. Give your clients the choice of using credit cards

Small businesses are being increasingly frequented by more and more people, because they are able to provide goods and services at affordable prices. Since you are looking to attract more clients, it is worth introducing some conveniences that will set your business apart from others.

One of these is to offer your clients the option of making their payments by credit card. A client can then feel free to drop by as and when he needs something, without having to worry about making payments in cash. Providing this facility will also tell your client that you care about his convenience and that you have confidence in his custom.

A growing number of small businesses have begun to accept payments by credit card. You as an entrepreneur will be required to open a merchant account to receive credit card payments, and you can do so without incurring much expense. In fact, you can even accept payments by credit card when you are running a home based small business enterprise.

This is definitely an idea that is worth considering as it will earn you plenty of popularity and provide convenience both for you and for your clients. Try it and see for yourself!

A Final Thought

So now that you have read these 121 Ideas, are you ready?

When you are looking to expand your business, you have to be completely focussed on marketing. And you have to maintain that kind of focus every single day, because you have to keep your hand in, so to speak. You cannot afford to lose touch.

So as you go about your business each day, remember to be on the lookout for marketing opportunities, so that you can make the most of every situation that presents itself.

Your business means everything to you and it is up to you to give it everything you've got. Only then can you expect to achieve the kind of returns that you would like. And that means that you must engage in at least one marketing activity every single day.

One day you may be meeting people at a social gathering, another day you could be attending a business lunch. On yet another day, it is entirely possible you could be meeting a new contact for the very first time. Whatever the occasion, never make the mistake of letting an opportunity pass you by.

Opportunities often turn up when you least expect them and the most unlikely situations can make a dramatic difference to the future of your business. So be vigilant and see that you don't miss out!

Best wishes and keep marketing your business!